Paddle
Scotland

An SCA Guide for Canoeists,
Kayakers and Paddleboarders

Pesda Press LTD

www.pesdapress.com

Proceeds from this guidebook will go to the
Andy Jackson Fund for Access

For further details about the fund, the projects it has supported,
and Andy Jackson, who inspired so many to go out and adventure
with friends, visit http://www.andyjacksonfund.org.uk/

Front cover – Connel Sound, Loch Etive / Photo: Tony Hammock
Back Cover – River Deveron near Huntley / Photo: Mike Forrester
           – Paddleboard yoga on the Union Canal / Photo: Shaune Walsh

2nd edition, completely updated and revised and renamed as Paddle Scotland, 2021
First published as Scottish Canoe Touring in Great Britain 2005 by Pesda Press
Tan y Coed Canol, Ceunant, Caernarfon
LL55 4RN, Wales

Copyright © 2005/2021 Scottish Canoe Association

Maps – Bute Cartographics Contains Ordnance Survey data
© Crown copyright and database right 2021

ISBN 9781906095758

Printed in Poland. www.lfbookservices.co.uk

Foreword

It hardly seems some 16 years since writing the Foreword to the first edition of this book, and it has been a pleasurable job revising and updating, and adding some new routes.

Since that time, paddle sports have boomed, and in addition to canoes and kayaks people are using inflatable canoes and kayaks, sit on tops and paddleboards – hence the change of emphasis and of the name from Scottish Canoe Touring to Paddle Scotland.

The book always set itself the task of pulling together routes on rivers, lochs, sea lochs, canals, and some sheltered coastlines to cater for those not taking part in white-water paddling. The routes will also satisfy those using inflatable canoes and kayaks, sit on tops and paddleboards.

It was always intended that the routes would offer itineraries from day tours up to multi-day canoe-camping expeditions. In addition, and a new departure for the book, we aim to help those who wish for only a relaxing day trip – or shorter – on water with no obstructions, portages or worries. These have been picked out in an easy-to-read way. There are also eleven suggested routes across Scotland coast to coast, to tempt the hardy.

Scotland has many different types of scenery and terrain, much of it easily accessed, and this is a wonderful way for paddlers to see wild countryside – one of the last left in Europe. Since 2005, with new access legislation, Scotland has offered great experiences to the traveller, and ease of access has drawn many to our shores.

As in earlier years, thanks are due to paddlers who wrote about their favourite waters, and as before, proceeds of the sale of this guidebook go to the Andy Jackson Fund for Access, a charity set up to remember a famous and generous international Scottish paddler, who died in 2004. The Fund supports projects in Scotland to further and promote access for paddlers.

I welcome you to Scotland and hope you enjoy paddling and holidaying here.

Eddie Palmer, Guidebook editor

Eddie Palmer   *Polly Pullar*

Contents

Far North

Thurso

Ullapool

Bonar Bridge

Inverness

West

Kyle of Lochalsh

Mallaig

Fort William

Oban

Lochgilphead

Cowal

East

Moray and Grampian

Tayside

Angus

Fife

Central

Central

South

Ayrshire

The Clyde Valley

Dumfries and Galloway

Borders

Cross Scotland Routes

Contents – Short Easy Trips

Far North

Mike Forrester

Passing
Place

Acknowledgements

Some of the waters in this book have been paddled by many people, and so three or four slightly different descriptions of the same river or loch have been helpful in order to get down on paper a rounded account of the enjoyment to be had. In some cases, there has only been a single account received. Thanks to all who contributed:

Duncan Black, Robin Cole, Fred Conacher, Mary Conacher, Paul Cromey, Roland Denereaz, Chris Dickinson, Anna Gordon, Steve Hankin, Richard Hathaway, John Hattersley, Paul Jackson, Stuart Marshall, Geoff Miller, Eddie Palmer, Jonathan Riddell, Dave Rossetter, Graeme Smith, Bridget Thomas, Malcolm Wield, Staff of YMCA Lakeside – Windermere, and Members of the Open Canoe Sailing Group.

Special thanks regarding the compilation of this guide to:

Mary Connacher, Eddie Palmer, John Picken, Stuart Smith, and Bridget Thomas.

Thanks to Jonathan Riddell for photo editing and for all those who submitted photos for use in this book. The photos used have been acknowledged in the captions.

Important Notice

Canoeing, kayaking and paddleboarding are healthy outdoor activities which always carry some degree of risk, as they involve adventurous travel, often away from habitation. Guidebooks give an idea of where to access a river, where to egress, the level of difficulty, and the nature of the hazards to be encountered. However, the physical nature of river valleys changes over time, water levels vary considerably with rain, and features such as weirs, walls and landings are changed by man. Trees block rivers, and the banks erode, sometimes quickly. Coastal sections, sea lochs and large inland lochs are subject to the effect of tides and weather.

This guidebook is no substitute for inspection, personal risk assessment and good judgement. You should be wary of paddling above your comfort zone and should seek instruction where necessary from any of the excellent providers we have in the UK. The decision on whether to paddle or not, and any consequences arising from that decision, remains yours and yours alone.

Using the Guide

The main aim of the guide is to help paddlers to go out safely into the countryside and onto the water, with a minimum of fuss and with basic helpful information.

It does not include white-water paddling of grade 3 and above, except for some stretches of river where such rapids are easily portaged, or carried around. The *Scottish White Water* publication describes these other rivers.

002 Middle Thurso

Number, Name and Icons

Dirlot Gorge

Section of river or outline of area

Length	12km
OS	11
Grade	2/3

Quick Reference information
May include tidal information if needed

Icons – types of water

 Canals.

 Inland lochs with no current or tide but which, in high winds, can produce large waves.

 Rivers where flood conditions can make paddling difficult, and requiring a higher level of skill. The rivers in this guide have grade 1 and 2 rapids.

 White water that despite being relatively easy and suitable for touring will require some skills and experience of white water, or require portages. Grade 2 and 3.

 Estuaries and sea lochs where the direction of flow of the tidal streams are all-important, and usually cannot be paddled against.

 Open sea, safer coastal routes suitable for placid water touring kayaks and canoes (**in calm, stable weather**).

The text points out the individual difficulties of the various waters. Readers are urged to look at (inspect) any water they are uncertain of, and to access up-to-date weather information. The mountains and lochs of Scotland are subject to frequent, sudden and local changes in weather due to the topography and prevailing weather patterns, and these should be regarded with great respect.

The guide is not intended for paddling on the sea in sea kayaks, which is outside its scope, although some popular coastal trips are included, where open canoes have been used frequently. Particular attention should be paid to weather forecasts when deciding if it's wise to undertake one of these journeys.

Using the Guide

Icons – other

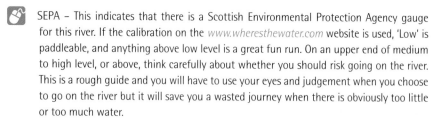

SEPA – This indicates that there is a Scottish Environmental Protection Agency gauge for this river. If the calibration on the *www.wheresthewater.com* website is used, 'Low' is paddleable, and anything above low level is a great fun run. On an upper end of medium to high level, or above, think carefully about whether you should risk going on the river. This is a rough guide and you will have to use your eyes and judgement when you choose to go on the river but it will save you a wasted journey when there is obviously too little or too much water.

Portages – Portaging is the carrying of canoes, kayaks or paddleboards. Portage distances have been restricted to the occasional 100m or so, around rapids, canal locks etc. These portages are generally along the length of the waterway, that is downstream, not over heights.

Beware! – This icon indicates that there are isolated dangers (described in more detail in the text). These should be carefully identified and evaluated by the reader.

Weirs – These are either very straightforward or extremely dangerous. The reader should inspect and if in doubt portage.

Expedition routes – Some of the five geographical sections also contain suggested expedition routes. Only bare details are included, as good planning and provisioning would be required, with the ability to survive in the outdoors for several days. Where routes cross the watershed, fairly near to the west coast, severe weather conditions can be encountered. Portages are often long and hard, both in terms of length, and height required, and thought should be given to support teams, and the means of communication with them.

Short Easy Trips – This icon indicates that a section is included which is recommended for those seeking a half-day or short-day paddle. The reader will be able to devise many more to suit their particular needs by studying and breaking up the longer tours described.

Quick Reference

Length – The distances indicate the full extent of the paddling available. Shorter journeys can be planned in most (but not all) cases.

OS – Indicates the number(s) of the Ordnance Survey 1:50,000 Landranger Series needed to cover the route described.

Grades – On rivers the grades of water are indicated using the international standard (see over).
2 would indicate grade 2 sections.
1–2 means harder than 1 but easier than 2.
1/2 means that stretches of 1 and stretches of 2 may be encountered.
(3) would indicate an isolated short stretch of grade 3 that could be avoided by portaging.

Tides - Basic tidal information such as whether tidal streams are negligible or strong, or whether the area dries out at low water. If needed there will be more detail in the main text.

Position

Positions are given in the form of six-figure Grid References (for Ordnance Surevey maps); followed by Latitude and Longitude to 2 decimal places (for GPS and Sat Nav systems).

E.g.   (NM 697 728; 56.7896, -5.7769)

River Grading

Rivers are graded in difficulty by an agreed international standard, and a simplified version is quoted here.

Grade 1   Easy. Occasional small rapids or riffles, waves regular and low. Most appropriate course, with deepest water, easy to see from canoe or kayak and steer down. Obstacles, e.g. pebble banks, very easy to see. These present no real problems to paddlers able to steer canoes and kayaks. Steering is needed, especially on narrow rivers.

Grade 2   Medium. Fairly frequent rapids, usually with regular waves, easy eddies, and small whirlpools and boils. The course is generally easy to recognise, but may meander around gravel banks and trees, etc. Paddlers may get wet.

Grade 3   Difficult. Rapids are numerous, and can be continuous. Course more difficult to see and decide, landing in order to inspect may be wise. Drops may be high enough not to see water below, with high and irregular waves, broken water, eddies and whirlpools / boils. No water with rapids of above grade 3 is advised or included in this guide. Where there are grade 3 rapids, avoiding or portaging is always possible.

Grade 4   Very Difficult. Long and extended stretches of rapids with high, irregular waves, difficult broken water, strong eddies and whirlpools. Course is often difficult to recognise. High falls, inspection from bank nearly always necessary.

Grade 5   Exceedingly Difficult. Long and unbroken stretches of white water, with individual features and routes very difficult to see. Submerged rocks, high waterfalls, falls in steps, exceptionally difficult whirlpools and fast eddies. Previous inspection definitely necessary, risk of injury, swims always serious.

Grade 6   Absolute limit of difficulty. All previous mentioned difficulties increased to limit of practicability. Definite risk to life.

River Levels

In this guide, an indication is given of a suitable level to paddle by simple viewing on-site, for example 'if the rocks are covered downstream from the bridge'. Most of the rivers described can be easily seen from a road or bridges, and judgements on level are reasonably easy to make by the individual.

The SCA website (*www.canoescotland.org*) also has an invaluable service offered, together with SEPA (the Scottish Environmental Protection Agency) and Visit Scotland, of live river levels from gauges on mostly the smaller rivers. Common sense will aid the paddler to make judgements on the levels in the larger rivers. For example, if several tributaries of the Tay are 'huge', then within a few hours, the Tay itself will also be very high.

In addition, the SCA website contains a wealth of information on the paddler's environmental responsibilities in an age where these have become even more pressing and urgent. This applies to all activities, and especially to wild camping, the standard of which leads to all of us being judged on our behaviour.

The now long-standing SOAC (Scottish Outdoor Access Code) is also fully explained.

SCA Where's the Water

Where's the Water is the website which takes river gauge readings from SEPA and calibrates them for paddlers. The calibration process is manual and subjective, and is a work in progress. There are some gauges with no calibrations and some with out of date calibrations. The site relies on submissions from paddlers to keep it up to date and accurate. Whenever you paddle a section of river consider which level you feel it should be calibrated at in your opinion as a paddler: Empty, Scrape, Low, Medium, High, Very High or Huge. Then submit this to the site using the form linked below the map. Even submissions which confirm that the section is calibrated accurately are useful. Find it on the SCA website: *www.canoescotland.org*

Hydro Campaign

Currently, there is a threat to some of Scotland's upland rivers by a myriad of small hydro-electric schemes, contributing to the country's renewable energy targets. These could stop some rivers from being paddled at all, and lead to lower flows. For details, see the excellent and revamped SCA website: *www.canoescotland.org*

Access

The Land Reform (Scotland) Act 2003 now gives a clear framework for everybody to enjoy outdoor sports and activities. The Scottish Canoe Association and NatureScot (formally SNH), the relevant government agency, have produced a leaflet outlining both rights, and, as importantly, responsibilities (reproduced below).

It is important that everybody realises the two-way responsibility inherent in this Act, one of the best in Europe. Much of this is common sense, so overall ... think!

There is now a statutory right of access to most land and inland water in Scotland. The Scottish Outdoor Access Code explains how to do this.

Enjoying responsible access on land

Access disputes have often arisen concerning either vehicle parking, or crossing land to reach water. Respect people's privacy by staying away from houses and private gardens – access rights do not apply here. Be discreet when either changing, or going to the toilet. If you are wild camping, choose a spot well away from roads and buildings, and be sure to remove all traces of your camp. Camp in small numbers, for a maximum of two or three nights. Do not use road lay-bys, or car parks.

Access rights do not apply to motorised transport – do not use private (usually estate) roads without permission, and do not drive over rough country, as environmental damage might occur. Take care with parking, and do not block access or tracks or farm gates. You do, however, have a right, when not interfering with other people's livelihood or pleasure, to walk with a canoe from the road to the river or loch. Obviously, don't damage walls, fences, hedges or gates. Try and avoid animals and growing crops by keeping to the edge of fields, watch for any advice signs, and follow any reasonable guidance given.

Enjoying responsible access to water

Access rights apply to inland water such as rivers, lochs, canals, and reservoirs.

- Respect the needs of anglers – avoid rods, lines, and other tackle. When close to anglers, keep noise and disturbance to a minimum.

- Care for the environment – do not disturb wildlife, plants or your surroundings. Do not pollute the water, and report any pollution or suspicious activity.

- Rivers – watch out for anglers, pass with least disturbance, and try to attract attention from upstream. If possible, wait for a signal to proceed and then follow a route down indicated if it is safe and practicable to do so.

- Lochs – if anglers are present, try and keep a safe distance away to avoid any contact and disturbance. If the water is part of a commercial fishery, and intensively used, always attempt to speak to the land manager before going on the water.

- Sea – the sea is open and free, but take care to avoid disturbing nesting birds and other wildlife. For example, seals are lovely to paddle near, but do not stress nursing mother seals and pups. There are many sea lochs in this guide where access poses no problem at all.

- Canals – be aware of other traffic, and avoid motorised craft, who often do not have the draft (depth in the water) to avoid you. Access rights do not apply through locks and lifts. Follow any regulations and guidance, and if in doubt – ask. The canals in this guide have a very useful and informative website.

- Reservoirs and hydro schemes – avoid going too close to water intake points, spillways, or other hydro infrastructure. Remember that water levels may change very quickly, and without warning.

Key Principles

Your main responsibilities are to:

- Care for the environment

- Take responsibility for your own actions

- Respect the interests of other people

These principles apply equally to canoeists, anglers, other water users, and land managers.

Local Authorities / National Park Authorities' Responsibilities

These Authorities have a responsibility to uphold access rights. If you feel you are challenged unreasonably, or otherwise prevented or discouraged from enjoying your access rights, you should report it to the relevant Access Officer (who will usually be employed in the Planning Department).

Land Managers' Responsibilities

Land Managers must respect access rights in their day-to-day work. Sometimes, for health and safety, or animal welfare reasons, they may have to lock gates or suggest alternative routes around areas of work. Co-operating with such situations helps land managers to work safely. Anglers are asked to respect access rights and to allow canoes to pass at the earliest opportunity.

Extra advice to canoeists

Please pay special regard to parking on rivers or lochs, and do not park in passing places on single-track roads. This causes much annoyance to local people. Remember that parking for a van and canoe trailer requires more space than for a small car, and park with consideration.

While driving on single-track roads, pay heed to the good practice prevalent, and allow overtaking by faster traffic (you can incur penalties for obstruction if you do not do this!), and pull into passing places in good time, avoiding the need for any reversing of trailers.

For more information on the Act, the Access Code, and contact details for Access Officers:

www.outdooraccess-scotland.com   *www.canoescotland.org*

River Advisers

The major rivers in this guidebook have River Advisers. They are happy to be contacted for information about likely river flows, any particular local access issues (avoiding the annoyance of other water-users), or new hazards. You can help them by reporting anything of note that you find on your trip. Please remember that it is a voluntary service, and that River Advisers have other jobs – be sensitive about the times you contact them. You are under no obligation to contact a River Adviser, but planning a long trip with a large group might repay itself by contacting them. The major touring rivers can come under particular pressure at times. There is a list of River Advisers on the SCA website www.CanoeScotland.com.

SCA Access and Environment Policy Committee

The aim of this guidebook and the aims of the Access Committee are the same: to assist you to enjoy Scottish water. Broadly this gives us two areas of work. The practical day-to-day resolution of local issues is complemented by the provision of information, advice and other action to promote enjoyment of the countryside.

The Land Reform (Scotland) Act and the Access Code which came into force on 9th February 2005 have enabled the Committee to take a much broader view of our work. When arguing for our rights we now have a legal framework which we helped to write. The Access Code provides the framework to resolve the practical day-to-day issues that will occur on and off the water. It forms the basis of the Paddlers' Code and our negotiations with land managers and local authorities, particularly their Access Officers. These negotiations range from sensitive areas on the river to parking, toilets, information signs, camping provision, gates, fences, etc. Other important areas of negotiation include improving access to existing hydro schemes and limiting the damage caused by new ones. All is aimed at facilitating access to Scotland's water and giving you the information you may need to use access responsibly.

This legal right enables us to look much more widely at helping paddlers enjoy the Scottish countryside. Using our Environmental Policy we promote canoeing as an environmentally sound as well as healthy activity – an ideal recreational activity. Come and join us.

Loch Assynt 📷 Tim Har

Far North

Contents

Thurso

Ullapool

Bonar Bridge

Inverness

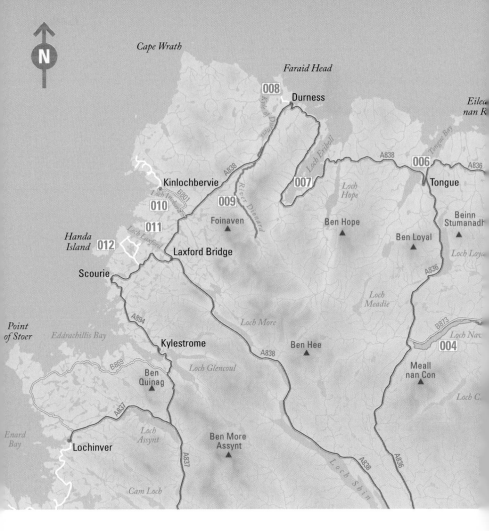

Thurso

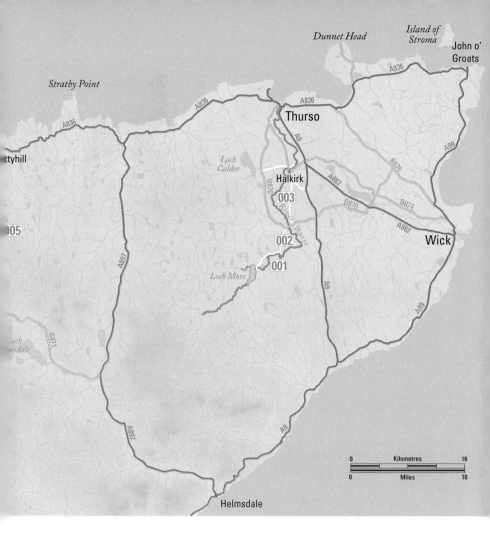

Loch Laxford   📷 Sue Tadman

River Coigach   📷 Jonny Hawkins

Lower Thurso ⬚ *Colin Matheson*

Thurso

This area has two main towns, Wick and Thurso, the latter best known for its surfing beaches. Caithness is flatter and more agricultural than its western and southern neighbours, which often comes as a surprise to visitors. The east coast has a string of pretty fishing villages and inland is the famous 'Flow Country', one of the largest areas of blanket bog in Europe. To the west is a vast empty land with no settlements of any size.

The main event in this part of the world in recent years has been the advent of the NC (North Coast) 500 route, which promotes the road route around the north of Scotland from Inverness, in a clockwise direction. The roads have always been there – now there is the addition of a lot more traffic. This is a mixed blessing; good for the local economy but one is likely to meet far more vehicles, many not driven well.

River Thurso

This is the most north-easterly river on the UK mainland, and flows gently from a bog south-west of Thurso town. It is probably little paddled, has quiet rather than spectacular scenery, and is a popular salmon river. The river is

small until it passes through Loch More, which can be reached by a public road from the A895, the main spine road running north up to Thurso. There is one stretch of continuous rapids, the Dirlot Gorge, grade 2/3 (a good grade 3 in high water), and large grade 3 rapids in the villages of Westerdale and Halkirk. A start below Halkirk avoids rapids. The guide to the river is presented in three sections.

001 Upper Thurso

Length	5km
OS	11
Grade	1

Water level

There is a gauge in Halkirk, 24 inches is a good level.

Access

Road access and parking are easy, as this is a quiet part of the country. This first section can be accessed at the outlet of Loch More (ND 083 461; 58.3937, -3.5707), with egress further down the road (ND 117 481; 58.4123, -3.5133).

Campsites & accommodation

There are two sites in Thurso, which is a fairly major town.

Description

Km

0   Bridge at Lochmore Cottage, exit from loch. The small Loch Beg follows.

3.5 Strathmore Lodge on left bank.

5   River leaves road. Take out here (ND 117 481; 58.4123, -3.5133), or carry on down next section.

002 Middle Thurso

Dirlot Gorge

Length	12km
OS	11
Grade	2/3

Access

Start where river leaves minor road at ND 117 481; 58.4123, -3.5133. Egress at Westerdale Bridge, B870 (ND 131 518; 58.4458, -3.4907), or to avoid a long flat paddle, take out on a track at ND 133 490; 58.4207, -3.4862, after 4km of fast water. (The grade 2/3 stretch is continuous grade 3 in high water).

Description

Km

0   River leaves road. Series of small drops.

1   Dirlot Castle ruin on left bank. Start of rapids, small ledges and bedrock rapids.

7   Cemetery on bank, last rapid, large rock in the middle.

8   Farm road bridge.

9   Two brochs on right bank.

12   Dale Moss bog on right side. Broch on

right followed by road bridge, B870 – Westerdale.

003 Lower Thurso

Length	25km
OS	11
Grade	1/2 (3)

Access

Westerdale Bridge (NC 131 518; 58.4145, -5.2042), egress Thurso Road Bridge (NC 118 681; 58.5601, -5.2399).

Description

Km

0   B870 road bridge and Westerdale hamlet. Large grade 3 rapid below bridge. More small hamlets follow on both banks.

9   Railway bridge – Georgemas Junction Station is 3km to right, where the rail line divides, with branches to both Wick and Thurso. Rapids start for next 2km.

10   Weir. Start of a continuous kilometre of grade 2 white water.

10.5 B874 road bridge, and Halkirk village.

11   Weir. Braal Castle.

17   Rail bridge.

21.5 Weir.

25   Thurso Road Bridge (NC 118 681; 58.5601, -5.2399).

004 Loch Naver

Length	9km
OS	16

Introduction

This area of the far north is wild and spectacular, and mainly unexplored by paddlers. The scenery is very fine and people, apart from anglers, are few and far between.

Access

The loch (NC 57 35; 58.2803, -4.4415 to NC 66 38; 58.3101, -4.2897) can be accessed from the north side off the B873, and offers a suitable short wilderness paddle, from the west end and back.

Description

Loch Naver runs for 9km east from Altnaharra on the A836, a long and tortuous single-track road. To the south are the imposing crags of Ben Klibreck.

005 River Naver

Length	30km
OS	10/16
Grade	2

Introduction

The river is very shallow and stony, with frequent minor rapids, and quite dangerous due to many trees in high water. Strathnaver is of historic interest, being the scene of some of Scotland's most notorious land clearances in the 19th Century.

Water level

Drive along and have a look – the river comes up and down quickly.

Access

The B873 road follows the river all the way down, and so access on and off is quite easy. Access at the top, either off a farm road to just where the river leaves Loch Naver (NC 669 378; 58.3085, -4.2742), or off the B873 (NC 676 386; 58.3159, -4.2627). Final egress at A836

road bridge just before Bettyhill (NC 710 602; 58.5108, -4.2168).

Campsites & accommodation

There is a campsite at Bettyhill, where the Naver joins the sea.

006 Kyle of Tongue

Length	6km
OS	10
Tides	Tidal streams are weak

Introduction

The north coast is an extremely dangerous and exposed one, offering sheltered touring in only a couple of places.

The Kyle is a beautiful place, with villages around the western entrance from the sea.

Access

The A838 crosses part of the Kyle by a causeway. Access either off this via two parking places (NC 581 586; 58.4924, -4.4374), or by the minor road north, up the west side, to Talmine and Portvasgo (Talmine Bay NC 586 627; 58.5294, -4.4313).

Campsites & accommodation

There is a small site at Talmine, near the beach.

Short easy trip

Talmine harbour to Rabbit Islands (in settled weather) – 4km return.

Description

Talmine has a safe anchorage, used by yachts coming 'around the corner' making for Orkney, plus a village store and a campsite. In summer, this area is swarmed over by camper vans from Europe, who obviously have a good guidebook!

The Rabbit Islands offshore are good to make for in settled weather, with its own population of seals, but please do not disturb – this is a wild area. In very calm weather even Eilean nan Ròn could be attempted. This island was once inhabited and has ruined houses. In the 1970s a group of hippies repopulated it for a few years.

It is 7km from Talmine up the Kyle, under the causeway, to Tongue itself. Both Ben Loyal and Ben Hope are visible, usually, to the south.

The islands and coves at the entrance to the Kyle are frequently visited by whales and otters.

007 Loch Eriboll

Length	20km
OS	9
Tides	Tidal streams negligible

Introduction
The lochs of Eriboll and the Durness area are the only other part of the north coast offering anything to the non-sea kayaker.

Access
From the A838 on the western side of the loch, near where a burn enters the loch at its head (NC 391 547; 58.4508, -4.7607), and at the car park above the beach at Tràigh Allt Chàilgeag (NC 443 655; 58.5496, -4.6789).

Campsites & accommodation
Durness, 20km away.

Description
The inner part of Loch Eriboll is usually sheltered from the weather, and a trip can be undertaken from the head of the loch or near its mouth. At the head is the tidal lagoon of Lochan Havurn and sandy beaches. The west side is 9km up to the beach is open to the sea. The island of Eilean Choraidh sits in the middle of the loch.

Short easy trip
A more sheltered trip can be had by staying in the inner part of the loch, leaving from where a burn enters the loch at its head (NC 391 547; 58.4508, -4.7607), and returning to the same place.

008 Kyle of Durness

Length	16km
OS	9
Tides	Estuary empties at LW

Introduction
A pleasant area to spend a day, with the village of Durness and the 'craft village' of Balnakeil, rather incongruously based in a World War 2 military base. Minibus trips can be made to Cape Wrath (the only way to reach it, apart from by kayak).

Access
From the A838 down to the coast at Balnakeil village (NC 391 687; 58.5764, -4.7706), or from the same road as it skirts the eastern side of the Kyle (NC 38 65; 58.5428, -4.7869).

Campsites & accommodation
Available at Durness.

Description
To the west, launching west of the dunes of Faraid Head at Balnakeil gives access to Eilean Dubh, and then round into the Kyle of Durness. This is a pleasant but tidal estuary which empties at low water. It is 8km up to the head of the Kyle, when tides allow.

Other important points

A ferry crosses halfway up, to take passengers over towards a minibus on the west side heading for Cape Wrath. Offshore here can be dangerous, as it is an RAF bombing range.

009 River Dionard

Length	5km
OS	9
Grade	1/2 (3-)

Introduction

This is a small river giving some different paddling in the area, flowing down the wide Strath Dionard, with mountains either side. Mostly grade 1/2, but the little gorge near the end might be a touch harder.

Water level

The river needs to obviously have enough water in to paddle under the road bridge near the end. This is also a good place to inspect the rapids and small drops.

Access

Follow the A838 south up the strath from the head of the Kyle, passing a bridge over the river after 1km. In another 3km, at a house called Carbreck (NC 333 593; 58.4899, -4.8635), a track leaves on the left, reaching the river after 1km (NC 338 586; 58.4838, -4.8544). Parking is easy on rough ground, egress is best on the right, 1km after reaching the tidal Kyle (NC 372 634; 58.5282, -4.7995).

Campsites & accommodation

Available at Durness.

Description

The river starts with occasional easy rocky rapids and fast bends. At one point it obviously narrows, and becomes a touch harder with a few drops, dropping faster under the road bridge, and then suddenly coming to an end. The Kyle is sandy underneath, and egress is to the right on to the road.

010 Loch Inchard

Length	12km
OS	9
Tides	Tidal streams negligible within loch

Introduction

Loch Inchard is the first inlet coming south from Cape Wrath, and offers the first shelter for shipping.

Access

From Kinlochbervie, a small fishing port (NC 221 563; 58.4586, -5.0535), 6km along a narrow road from the A838 at Rhiconich, or from Rhiconich (NC 255 523; 58.4241, -4.9921) itself.

Campsites & accommodation

At Durness to the north, or Scourie, 15km south.

Description

It is 6km up to Rhiconich, and the entrance from the sea is very Norwegian fjord-like. Kinlochbervie stands in a wonderfully sheltered position, in a side loch off to the north, with port facilities for yachts and fishing boats, and shops etc.

Other important points

It's possible, in very calm weather, to launch on the west side of the village into Loch Clash, and paddle up the coast for 3km, within various islands to the beach at Oldshoremore. The walk from the end of the minor road to the north, up to Sandwood Bay, is very rewarding, considered one of the most famous and secluded beaches in Scotland.

011 Loch Laxford

Length	18km
OS	9
Tides	Tidal streams negligible within loch

Introduction
Loch Laxford is a wonderful area for exploring, and offers paddling in a sheltered loch in spectacular scenery.

Access
You can launch either at the head of the loch, off the main A838 road, at a boathouse where the road turns north away from the loch (NC 228 478; 58.3827, -5.0349); or at Fanagmore on the south side (NC 178 498; 58.3985, -5.1220), reached by minor roads.

Campsites & accommodation
At Scourie, 10km south.

Description
All of the islands, some of them very close to the shore with narrow passages are worth exploring, and seals and otters abound. In the northern extension of Loch a'Chad-Fi there is an outdoor school at Ardmore – if landing, ask permission. A round day trip of some 18km can be worked out.

Short easy trip
A there-and-back trip exploring the islands from either of the two access points is recommended.

Other important points
The River Laxford can be paddled for 5km from the western end of Loch Stack down to Laxford Bridge. It is a grade 2–3, and very narrow in places.

012 Handa Island

Length	3km
OS	9
Tides	Tidal streams strong

Tides and weather
This trip is best attempted at Neap tides, due to quite a strong flow both through the Sound of Handa, and also off the west coast. Tides reach 2–3 knots in both areas at Springs. An area to be avoided in any high winds, as it is very exposed to the north and west.

Description
From Tarbet, 1.5km from Fanagmore, a trip out to Handa Island can be made to one of the premier bird sanctuaries for Scotland. Car parking can be had where the ferry leaves for Handa (NC 164 488; 58.3890, -5.1452). Please note that you will be asked to pay a landing fee on Handa which is owned by the Scottish Wildlife Trust (beach at NC 148 476; 58.3775, -5.1716). The passage is normally a sheltered 1.5km.

Other important points
Many paddlers have circumnavigated Handa, but very calm conditions are needed for this.

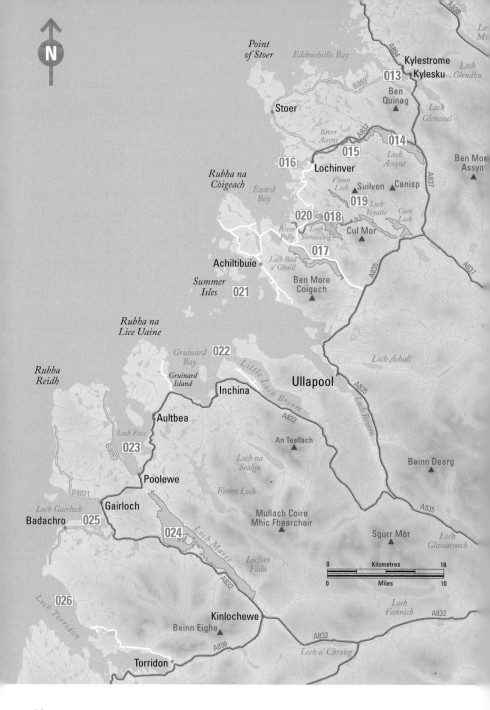

Entering Fionn Loch with Cul Mor in backgound　　　　　📷 *Steve Green*

Ullapool

Ullapool

This fishing village has expanded to be a major ferry port for Stornoway, and a centre for walking and climbing. It is always lively in the summer, and the Ceilidh Place Hotel offers frequent live music, and a bookshop, as well as political discussions. Ullapool is well served by hotels, B&Bs and restaurants.

013 Kylesku Area

Lochs Glencoul, Glendhu, and coast

Looking SW, Kylesku Bridge   📷 *Sonja Anderson*

Length	41km
OS	9/15
Tides	Tidal streams negligible within lochs

Introduction

Superlatives abound when discussing this part of Scotland, but it carries on with this superb area. I had a holiday with friends here some years ago where, in perfect summer conditions, we paddled open canoes on the sea for seven days running.

Tides

Tidal streams are strong in the narrows under the bridge. Within the area east of the road bridge, tides have little effect.

Access

A base at Kylesku, on the A894 north-south main road offers the paddler many day trips. Kylesku still has its old ferry slipways, made redundant by the bridge built in the late 1970s, and the southerly one is conveniently near the hotel (NC 230 338; 58.2572, -5.0207).

Campsites & accommodation

Scourie, 15km north. Drumbeg, along the coast to the west, has a seasonal campsite.

Short easy trips

Kylesku into Lochs Glencoul and Glendhu and return – up to 12km. Settled weather required.

Description

The way inland and to the south explores Loch Glencoul, and at its head is the highest waterfall in Britain, Eas a Chual Aluinn (NC 280 278; 58.2053, -4.9310). The way in by canoe is much more pleasant than the quite rough and boggy walk 5km in from the road, where you end up seeing the top of the fall, but not the full extent of it! The head of the loch, inside Loch Beag, provides many sheltered picnic sites. If you make the trip on a wet day the waterfall is spectacular. The round trip from Kylesku is 13km.

Loch Glendhu to the east could be combined in a day out as well, 12km up here and back. Out to sea, Eddrachillis Bay has many islands and sheltered waters. Loch a' Chàirn Bhàin offers a first 6km of shelter. Going north, islands can be wound around as far as the tiny beach at Upper Badcall, which is a further 7.5–8km (NC 153 415; 58.3231, -5.1582).

The West has more delights – possibly 8km (in a straight line) to the eastern side of Oldany Island. On the way the fjord-like Loch na Droighniche (NC 16 34; 58.2561, -5.1402) and

Loch Ardbhair (NC 16 33; 58.2471, -5.1394) after 3km. Then Loch Nedd (NC 13 32; 58.2369, -5.1898) a further 5km round to its head amongst lush woodland, and after that the useful Loch Dhrombaig (NC 11 33; 58.2450, -5.2247), with the village of Drumbeg, pub, and car parking, for a vehicle shuttle via the B869, one of Scotland's no-no roads for caravans. The coast after this becomes complicated and very indented, Culkein Drumbeg offering very sheltered but shallow anchorages for larger boats. It is not advised to go further around Oldany. The west side of the island is very exposed to the west and to the seas which come around the corner from the Point of Stoer, one of the west of Scotland's major headlands.

Overall, this part of the coast, both north and south of Kylesku, can offer a wonderful variety of day trips, or days of canoe-camping.

River Inver   Ⓒ *Jonny Hawkins*

Loch Assynt and River Inver

These two can be combined for a lovely day trip, in spectacular mountain scenery, and on easy water.

014 Loch Assynt

Length	9km
OS	15

Description

The prevailing wind is often from the west, and so the itinerary would be commencing off the A 837 road, to paddle west to east, The start point is where the loch is near the road at Little Assynt, and before the loch drops over the dam into the river (NC 156 248; 58.1734, -5.1397). The great bulk of Quinag will be on one's left all the time, and the loch will gradually open out to show the view to the east.

The mountains around Ben More Assynt to the south east are some of the hardest terrain for walkers in Scotland.

Eventually, the ruins of Ardvreck Castle will be seen on the left bank, most often in the summer with coachloads of tourists taking photos. Parking on ground by the road before the castle is usually easier (NC 242 237; 58.1671, -4.9926).

015 River Inver

Length	5km
OS	15
Grade	1–2

Introduction

The River Inver has a few pleasant kilometres before it suddenly changes character into a major white water undertaking of grade 4/5.

Description

The access is just downstream from the loch outflow (NC 154 251; 58.1760, -5.1434), and the river winds around bends away from the road, with tiny rapids and shallows.

The egress is where the river runs alongside a short piece of disused road that gives the opportunity for parking and picnics (NC 132 246; 58.1706, -5.1804). Downstream, the first of many fishing walls is visible. Don't miss the get-out, it is serious white water below here!

016 Stoer and Lochinver

Length	up to 35km
OS	15
Tides	Tidal streams negligible

Introduction

This bay between the Point of Stoer and the headland of Rubha Coigach to the south provides a number of canoeing and kayaking possibilities, with interesting indented fjord-like inlets, but obviously exposure seawards.

Access

The A837 is a fast main road into Lochinver (European-funded, to move fish southwards quickly), but the minor roads both north and south from Lochinver are single-track, winding, and very slow, especially in summer.

Campsites & accommodation

Clachtoll, Achmelvich and Port a Bhaigh at Altandhu, on the Achiltibuie road.

Description

South from the Point of Stoer (well worth visiting for spectacular cliffs and the stack of Old Man of Stoer) is the Bay of Stoer (NC 03 28; 58.1967, -5.3569) at the village of Clachtoll, with a campsite, and then Achmelvich (NC 058 247; 58.1683, -5.3064), with its own sandy bay campsite. This is laid-back summer holiday territory. Loch Roe, a fjord-like inlet, follows to the south. The headlands between the bays can be rounded, as always, in settled weather. Lochinver is the main settlement, with its own sea loch, 4km out to Soyea Island at the mouth.

Onwards south from Lochinver are more inlets and islands, offering more shelter from westerly or south-westerly winds. The coast road is a famous route of hairpins and steep gradients, banned to caravans, and difficult in places for trailers. Loch Kirkaig (NC 07 19; 58.1177, -5.2813) is pretty, and several other bays open up as minor burns reach the sea. It is a paddle of 9km over open sea to Achnahaird Bay, with a fabulous sandy beach on the peninsula to the south. Port a Baigh on the south side of the peninsula is the nearest campsite.

Recommended easy trips

The bays at Clachtoll (NC 040 271; 58.1890, -5.3391) and Achmelvich (NC 058 246; 58.1674, -5.3063).

017 The Inverpolly Lochs

Length	13km
OS	15
Grade	1

Portages

Two portages, one of which, necessary in normal low-water conditions, can be 1km long.

Loch Lurgainn   📷 *Tim Hamlet*

Introduction

Inland from Achnahaird is a string of lochs which give a pleasant day trip, with the backdrop of the peaks of the Inverpolly Nature Reserve. Best from the furthest east, in a westerly direction to the sea (downhill), although it has been done in the other direction (with some hard portages). The trip gives even a beginner the sense of a true wilderness trip, but with the road virtually alongside available for escape.

Water level

The small rivers between the three lochs can be dry in summer, but short rainstorms can bring the lochs and rivers up very quickly. Judge from the road.

Access

From the single track road which leaves the A835 at Drumrunie, west to Achnahaird and Achiltibuie. Access at east end from road (NC 139 068; 58.0113, -5.1543), egress onto same road at NC 039 130; 58.0626, -5.3289.

Campsites & accommodation

Port a Baigh at Altandhu
(www.portabhaigh.co.uk).

Description

Km

0   Start at easterly end of Loch Lurgainn. Parking on road in large passing-place (where climbers start out for Ben Mor Coigach). This is some 3.5km on the road to Achiltibuie, from where it leaves the A835. The burn then turns into the loch. There are spectacular mountains on both sides.

6   Short drop into Loch Bad na h-Achlaise, a very small loch. The loch bends to the right.

7   Fall into Loch Bad a' Ghaill, easy short portage over rocks.

9.5 Start of the Abhainn Osgaig, 1.5km river down to next loch. Shallow, with gravel rapids. If portaging, follow right bank, at first over a high piece of land, then by bank of river, where lining down may be possible.

11   Loch Osgaig.

13   Egress, on to road (NC 039 130; 58.0626, -5.3289), where there is a parking place. The loch then empties into a very short and rough river down to the sea over 250m.

Loch Sionascaig and Stac Pollaidh   📷 *Steve Green*   *Crossing into Loch Sionascaig*   📷 *Pete White*

018 Loch Sionascaig

Length	9km
OS	15

Portages
Northern access has a 0.5km portage. Southern access has a 200m portage.

Introduction
A lovely loch in a wild setting, it gives the impression of being miles from anywhere and takes the paddler into the heart of the Inverpolly National Nature Reserve.

Access
This loch can be accessed from the minor, and very winding, coastal B road north from the Stac Polly area to Lochinver. (Be careful of taking trailers on this road, it has very tight corners in places, which are being gradually improved). There are two access points, the easiest being north of the valley of the River Polly, (NC 082 136; 58.0698, -5.2565), from the road to Loch na Dàil, then upstream into the western arm of Loch Sionascaig. The other is 2km north (NC 093 151; 58.0838, -5.2390), along a path between Loch Cail an Uidhean and Loch Buine Moire, to Boat Bay on the main loch, a delightful enclosed bay with good campsites.

Be very careful with parking on this road as there are no obvious parking places!

Campsites & accommodation
Wild sites abound. Port a Baigh is the nearest formal site in this area.

Description
Loch Sionasgaig is 4.5km long and 3km wide, with Eilean Mor in the centre, another good campsite. At the eastern end, a narrow gap with a short river leads upstream to Lochan Gainmeich, and Loch an Doire Dhuibh.

Sunset on Fionn Loch   📷 *Steven Lindsay*

019 Loch Veyatie and Fionn Loch

Length	27km
OS	15
Grade	1

Portages

There is a portage of a waterfall after Cam Loch.

Introduction

Another true wilderness trip, but with no real difficulties and great views of Suilven.

Access

There is road access from the A835, 2km from Ledmore Junction, where the A837 and A835 join. Access the river where a tiny river flows under the road, just east of Elphin village (NC 229 120; 58.0616, -5.0058).

Campsites & accommodation

No formal sites are near, although Port a Baigh is west, and Kylesku is to the north. There are wild sites on the trip.

Description

The small river near Elphin gives access to the area (a much better option than the horrendous portage up the Kirkaig from the west). This gives entry to the Cam Loch, 3km long. Heading west, entry to Loch Veyatie is via a waterfall that will need portaging. Loch Veyatie is 7km long, and leads into the Uidh Fhearna, a short river, which in turn flows into Fionn Loch, 3.5km long. This route has the spectacular bulk of Suilven, one of Scotland's most recognisable mountains, to the north. The paddle in and back is well worthwhile.

The waterfall draining Cam Loch   📷 *Simon Raven*

020 Loch Veyatie to River Polly

Length	18km
OS	15
Grade	1–2

Portages

There are two portages, the first after Cam Loch, the other west out of Loch Veyatie, which is 2km including a short uphill, and a burn downhill.

Note (2020) – this route has been somewhat compromised by new deer fencing planned for the area of the second and long portage.

Introduction

An interesting variation on the two previous routes is a trip west, with a difficult portage, which has been done by kayak. (There are relatively few long trips going west on the west coast, due to the watershed being so near the coast).

Access

Access is via the A835 near Elphin, as in Route 19 (NC 229 120; 58.0616, -5.0058); egress can be after Loch Sionascaig as in access to Route 018 (NC 083 135; 58.0690, -5.2547).

Campsites & accommodation

Wild sites en route, with Port a Baigh near the finish.

Description

Take the route as described in Route 019. Then 5.5km down Loch Veyatie is a large bay on the left (west). Paddle up to the westerly end, and portage 250m north-west up to a burn leaving via a tiny lochan (NC 123 178; 58.1093, -5.1903). This is soon swollen by another burn leaving Loch a Mhadail. The burn flows for 1.5km down to Lochan na Claise, then by a very short burn down to the most easterly bay on Loch Sionascaig. The whole of the loch is then before you, and an exit can be made at the first access point in Route 18.

Horse Island, The Summer Isles　　　⬚ *Tim Hamlet*

the tiny port of Old Dornie, sheltered behind Isle Ristol.

Access

A minor road circles the Rubha Coigach peninsula, from either Achnahaird or Achiltibuie, and Old Dornie is 1km off this road (NB 982 112; 58.0439, -5.4241).

Campsites & accommodation

Altandhu, Polbain, and Achiltibuie all have accommodation. The nearest campsite is , Port a Baigh, very handy at Altandhu, often the start of a trip.

021 The Summer Isles

Length	16km
OS	15
Tides	Weak tidal streams

Distances

A round paddle of 16km circumnavigates both of the main islands.

Tides and weather

The tidal flow around the islands is variable, but with little appreciable effect – even at Springs, the tidal streams flow at a maximum of 0.5 knots. The area should be avoided in any high winds, as it is very exposed to the west.

Introduction

The Summer Isles are an interesting and pretty group of islands not far from Ullapool, at the mouth of Loch Broom. The distance over from the coast at Coigach, to the north, is a feasible kilometre of open water, if leaving from

Description

The usual destinations are Tanera Mor, the largest island, and Tanera Beg, its neighbour. The usual precaution of settled weather is a must here ... several times in the past, groups have left the mainland in calm conditions, only to be benighted by a change in the weather.

Tanera Mor is the only permanently inhabited island; on its east side is the natural harbour 'The Anchorage', with a jetty to the south, a fish farm in the centre, and a landing, post office and coffee shop to the north. On the north-west corner of the island is an interesting little cove, with a narrow slot through to the strait between the two islands. Tanera Beg has a fabulous small gap between it and Eilean Fada Mor to the north (unfortunately now nearly filled by another fish farm, and a boom). The entrance from the south has a coral sand bottom, clearly visible at low tide.

It is an undoubted privilege to paddle here. The circumnavigation of both islands is about 16km.

Other important points

The other islands are not mentioned because they are really a sea kayaker's domain.

022 Little Loch Broom and Gruinard Bay

Length	Up to 29km
OS	19
Tides	Tidal streams weak

Distances

A trip of 24km can be had in Little Loch Broom, and 4.5km in Gruinard Bay.

Tides

Within Little Loch Broom, tidal streams reach a maximum of 1 knot at Springs. They have little effect on a crossing to Gruinard Island.

Introduction

This area offers some wonderful paddling. The view to the south of Little Loch Broom is dominated by the massive bulk of An Teallach, one of the largest Munros. The view to the north, once out of the loch, is filled with the Summer Isles.

Access

There is access from the A832 coastal main road on to Little Loch Broom near its head (NG 08 88; 57.7861, -6.9250); and from the same road, on to the beach at Gruinard Bay via a parking place (NG 953 900; 57.8525, -5.4549).

Campsites & accommodation

Laide, west side of Gruinard Bay.

Description

It is 12km from the head of Little Loch Broom out to where the ferry crosses over to the alternative community of Scoraig, now also linked by a 4-wheel drive track.

The headland of Stattic Point round to Gruinard Bay can be too windy, but the bay is worth seeing for the beach at its head. The island of Gruinard, once famous as the 'anthrax island' due to biological experiments during World War 2, is now clear, and can be visited, 1.5km off Mungasdale Bay to the east, and 3km from the large beach.

Short easy trip

Gruinard Bay, to Gruinard Island and back – round trip of between 4 and 10km.

023 Loch Ewe

Length	Up to 24km round trip
OS	19
Tides	Tidal streams negligible within loch

Introduction

Loch Ewe is large and exposed to the north-west. It is also a live training area for warships, which can speed in and out of the loch, a facility which has been kept since World War 2 when Atlantic convoys gathered here.

Access

From Poolewe on A832 (NG 860 810; 57.7675, -5.6037).

Exploring the isles of Loch Maree   *Jim Wallis*

Campsites & accommodation
Available at Poolewe.

Description
Poolewe at the inner end is sheltered, and also near the Inverewe Gardens, with semi-tropical plants and well worth visiting. The loch is some 12km long, and rather featureless, although the old wartime fortifications on the west side at the end of the road are worth a look.

024 Loch Maree

Length	Up to 40km round trip
OS	19

Introduction
Loch Maree is one of the most mysterious and attractive lochs in north-west Scotland. It has islands about halfway down its length that are mostly bare rock, with pines. Some are sandy, and these are the heavily protected nesting sites of Great Northern Divers. In Spring time, please go to the Loch Maree Visitor Centre, on the main A832 road near the southern end of the loch for advice. It's worth learning about the wildlife and geology of the area anyway.'

Access
From the west side of the loch, from the A832, at or near the Loch Maree Hotel (NH 915 705;

57.6759, -5.5020), a parking place near the southern end of the loch (NH 001 650; 57.6305, -5.3530), or Forest Walk car park at (NG 889 721; 57.6890, -5.5470).

Campsites & accommodation
At Kinlochewe or Poolewe.

Description
The loch is yet another Scottish gem, being 20km long, with a variety of interesting islands in the centre where it is 3.5km wide. Slioch dominates the skyline to the north-east, but the whole area is surrounded by breathtaking mountains.

Short easy trip
Slatterdale to islands and back, a 4 to 10km round trip.

025 Loch Gairloch

Length	Up to 24km round trip
OS	19
Tides	Tidal streams negligible

Introduction
This loch is fairly isolated with regard to the coast north and south, but the shoreline of the loch is fairly long, with some interesting inlets. A good holiday can be had by using a centre such as the campsite at Poolewe, or one of the Gairloch ones, and exploring Lochs Ewe, Maree, Gairloch and Torridon. Inland there is a fabulous range of mountains.

Access
From the A832 up the eastern side of the loch (NG 80 76; 57.7197, -5.7000), or the minor road which goes west from Gairloch village along the north shore.

Campsites & accommodation
Around the loch, at Little Sands, Gairloch, Charlestown, or Kerrysdale.

Description
From the northern entrance to the loch, Big Sand, on Caolas Beag (NG 752 788; 57.7425, -5.7834), gives access to the shallow sound between the mainland and the island of Longa (campsite also at Little Sand Farm). It is 5km along the north shore to Gairloch village, road alongside. The coast turns south, with a beach, headland, and 3km round to Charlestown village. In the south-east corner are the useful sheltered inlets of Loch Kerry and Loch Shieldaig, with islets and wooded shores. To the west again, 4km round from Charlestown, is Badachro, with its friendly pub, and very sheltered anchorage behind Eilean Horrisdale.

Short easy trip
From Gairloch village to Loch Shieldaig and back – a round trip of 8km.

026 Loch Torridon

Length	Up to 20km round trip
OS	24
Tides	Tidal streams negligible within loch

Introduction
Torridon is another highly indented inlet, with an inner and outer loch, giving more possibilities in bad weather.

Access
From the A896, which skirts the south side of the loch, Shieldaig being the first settlement (NG 815 536; 57.5197, -5.6545), and the minor road which hugs the north shore to Torridon village (NG 899 563; 57.5479, -5.5165).

Loch Torridon   📷 *Steve Green*

Short easy trip
Upper Loch Torridon.

Description
Loch Torridon itself is open and exposed, with no road on its northern side. Loch Diabeg is a small inlet, with the village of Lower Diabeg (NG 798 599; 57.5753, -5.6887), and access to the water. It is 4.5km across to Loch a Chracaich on the south shore, where there is a road. The scenery is more barren, and countryside more isolated than the former sections to the north. Loch Torridon narrows just inshore from here, and Loch Shieldaig opens up to the south, 5km up to Shieldaig village.

The entrance to Upper Loch Torridon is less than half a kilometre wide. The upper loch is 8km long, ending at Torridon village. There are roads on both north and south shores, so there are possibilities here for sheltered paddling in breathtaking mountain scenery. More inlets on the south shore.

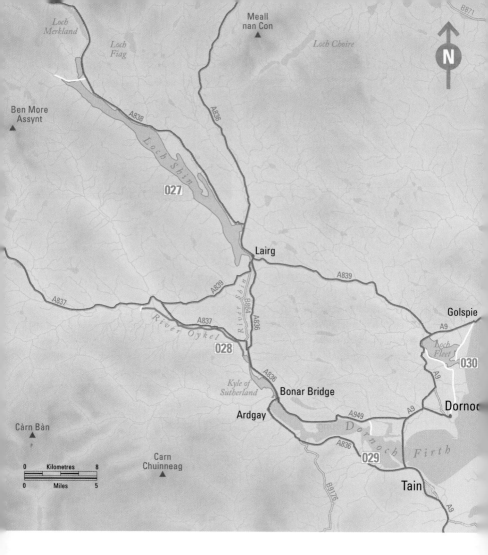

Bonar Bridge

Wading down a drop on the Upper Oykel   📷 *Graham Warren*

Bonar Bridge

Bonar Bridge does have a bridge ... a very important road bridge across the tidal Kyle of Sutherland, and it is a meeting of routes, but not much more, just a village.

027 Loch Shin

Length	Up to 28km
OS	16

Introduction

It's good to say something nice about every piece of water, but Loch Shin tries the patience! It is a very long loch, with almost no redeeming features, as the scenery is undulating with commercial forestry, much of it cleared and re-planted, with high deer fences. It is known to paddlers due to being part of one of the Cross-Scotland routes. The loch is much used for fishing from small boats, and is also very midge-ridden.

Access

The A838 runs down most of the north-east side of the loch giving numerous access points. At the southern end, a dam blocks direct exit to the village of Lairg. Take out before the dam on the left (north) side on to one of the short tracks used by anglers to reach the loch (NC 573 075; 58.0336, -4.4196).

Campsites & accommodation

There are wild sites on the loch and a formal site at Lairg.

Description

There are few features or settlements. A start may be had on Loch a Ghriama, to the north. This is connected to Loch Shin by a narrows which is crossed by a bridge (NC 390 252; 58.1862, -4.7418). The A838 runs down the north-east side. Lairg is a pleasant village, only 11km from Bonar Bridge, with the usual facilities.

Other important points

A B-road down the west side of the River Shin (grade 3), leads to the grade 4 Falls of Shin (Visitor centre and café – NC 576 991; 58.8557, -4.4716), well worth visiting in autumn to see the many salmon coming up to spawn, and jumping the falls.

028 Lower River Oykel and Kyle of Sutherland 🦫 🌊 🍂 🅂

Length	28km
OS	16/20/21
Grade	1–2
Tides	Strong tidal streams in estuary

Introduction

This trip gives a fairly fast river experience in a flat-bottomed and agricultural valley, becoming an easy tidal paddle for those not used to large estuaries. Mountain scenery gives way to the Kyle, which is pretty and wooded.

Access

From the A837 at Oykel Bridge, (NC 386 009; 57.9680, -4.7319) a minor road bridge 9km downstream (NC 460 013; 57.9742, -4.6070), and at Bonar Bridge on to the A9 (just upstream of bridge – NH 608 922; 57.8974, -4.3512).

Campsites & accommodation

At Lairg and Dornoch.

Description

The Oykel provides 9km of paddling, to add on to a trip down the Kyle of Sutherland. It is a flattish river of grade 1-2, in a flat-bottomed valley, but with mountains to the north and south.

Km

0 The start is just below Oykel Bridge, where the river flows under the main A837 major east-west route (NC 386 009; 57.9680, -4.7319). The high Falls of Oykel (grade 4–5) are just upstream. Downstream, on the east side of the bridge, is a track alongside the river for launching.

9 The next public road bridge at Inveroykel. The Oykel becomes tidal here, and usually known as the Kyle (so you need to time your journey so that you do this section on the outgoing tide).

10.5 The Cassley, a beautiful white water river, joins from the left.

13 Access and egress can be had where the road is alongside (NH 49 99; 57.9546, -4.5548).

21 The Shin joins from the left.

23 The main railway line to the north crosses the narrows. The Kyle has a widening out then a final narrow stretch before Bonar Bridge.

28 Bonar Bridge egress (just upstream of bridge – NH 608 922; 57.8974, -4.3512).

Short easy trip

Oykel Bridge to Bonar Bridge – 19km.

029 Dornoch Firth 🌊

Length	Up to 48km
OS	21
Tides	Strong tidal streams in narrows

Distances

48km from Bonar Bridge to Dornoch and return.

Introduction

This is a long, narrow firth with strong tides at the narrow parts (so you will need to work the tides so that the ingoing and outgoing are in your favour), and large sandbanks. It is possible to reach Dornoch around Dornoch Point in settled weather. Dornoch is renowned for good weather in summer, and has extensive beaches and sand dunes.

Access
From the A9, both sides of the firth. The north side is easier due to railway line on south side. East of Bonar Bridge (NH 61 90; 57.8778, -4.3466), and from Newton Point (NH 711 877; 57.8601, -4.1750).

Campsites & accommodation
At Lairg and Dornoch.

Description
It is 4km from Bonar Bridge to Wester Fearn Point and another 1.5km to Easter Fearn Point on the south bank, separated from a high point with Dun Creich fort on the north side by only 200m of water. Some 6km further on there is a turn to the south at Ardmore Point, and 4km further on the Dornoch Firth Bridge. The old ferry terminals are on points just before the bridge. It is 6km on to the open sea at Dornoch Point, with Tain to the south, and the town of Dornoch 2km along the coast to the north.

Other important points
East of the Dornoch Firth bridge, on the coastal route after Tain to Portmahomack is an artillery firing and bombing range, access not advised.

030 Loch Fleet

Length	8km round trip
OS	21
Tides	Estuary dries at LW

Introduction
This sheltered estuary lies to the north of Dornoch, and is a delightful, quiet wildlife habitat.

Access
The A9 runs across The Mound, a causeway at the landward end of the estuary. Minor roads run out on both sides of the stretch of water, offering easier parking, at Skelbo Castle to the south (NH 794 954; 57.9316, -4.0389), and Littleferry Pier (NH 805 956; 57.9337, -4.0204) to the north.

Campsites & accommodation
At Dornoch and Embo, just to the south.

Short easy trip
Good to paddle on a rising tide.

Description
The loch is only 4km long from The Mound, a causeway which the A9 road to the north crosses, to its mouth at Littleferry, the old ferry crossing in former times. The loch virtually dries out at low tide, but would be of interest to birdwatchers.

Other important points
From Loch Fleet to the north is the east coast of Sutherland, and the east Caithness coast, with rocky cliffs, no large inlets, and very little shelter.To the south of this area lies the Cromarty Firth, large, and partially industrial (it is used as a storage place for disused or de-commissioned oil rigs), the Moray Firth, used by large ships, and the Beauly Firth, very dry at low tide.

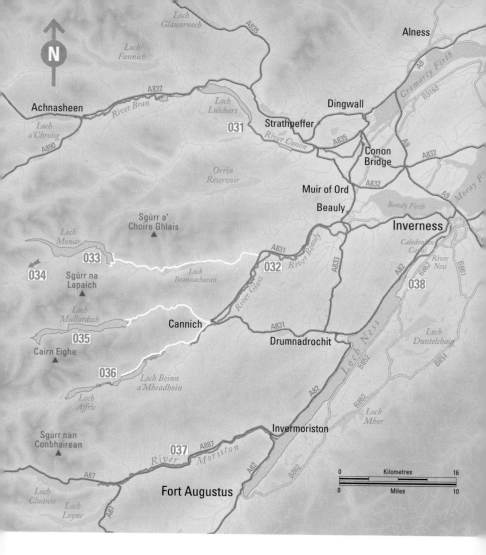

Inverness

River Conon   ⌾ *Eddie Palmer*

Inverness

Inverness is now a city, and a very fast-expanding centre for the north of Scotland. It is essentially an urban centre, but useful for shopping, and has backpacker accommodation, as well as the usual hotels and B&Bs. Several interesting glens come down to Inverness from the west and south.

031 River Conon and Upper Lochs

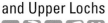

Length	53km
OS	25/20/26
Grade	1–2

Portages

Two portages of about 2km each.

Introduction

An interesting route, taking 2–3 days because of the portages. This route takes the paddler down from Achnasheen on the A832, east to Conon Bridge near Dingwall on the Cromarty Firth.

Water level

The River Bran needs to be inspected from the A832 to determine its level ... it is usually deep enough to paddle.

Access

Access point at NH NH 143 559; 57.5549, -5.1080 at the western end of Loch Gowan on the A890, west of Achnasheen. The A832 runs alongside much of the rest of the route.

Egress at A862 road bridge (NH 143 559; 57.5549, -5.1080), near Conon Bridge village.

River Bran 📷 *Jonny Hawkins*

Campsites & accommodation

This is an expedition involving wild campsites. Fortunately they are available nearly everywhere on this route.

Description

Km

0 Western end of Loch Gowan. Access point at NH 143 559; 57.5549, -5.1080.

4.5 River Bran leaves eastern end of loch.

5.5 Road bridge, Achnasheen village, burn joins on right. A flat river, down a flattish valley – road and railway on north side.

18.5 The very winding river enters Loch Achanalt – exit from loch difficult to see, around a left-hand bend.

20 After a railway bridge, after 2km where Loch a Chulinn narrows, portage on to road on left bank. The next 2km have a barrage, weirs, and power station.

24 Re-enter water 0.5km before a railway bridge. Loch Luichart then commences.

32.5 End of Loch Luichart – portage out on left bank. Portage is of 2km along road on left bank to the power station below the Lochluichart Dam. (If there is water, you might well see many kayakers trying to commit suicide on the very difficult stretch of the Conon, up to grade 5 here).

34.5 On the river! (Conon).

39 Loch Achonachie.

41 Dam – portage right. The Conon now behaves more like a normal lowland river.

45 Moy Bridge.

49.5 Weir, and a large island. Vegetation makes this next part a bit confusing. The left fork of the river is not possible at the time of writing (2020). Keep right as you follow the dam wall closely to your left. This channel becomes more and more narrow, stay in control as river quickens. As the woodland opens out quite a bit, look for a gap in the weir, and a drop to your left. This drop is fairly harmless, but the tail heads straight for another weir wall. You need to either break out to your left, and then cross the tail, or take a sharp turn to the right, downstream. You are now safe! Inspection is difficult before attempting the whole stretch.

52.5 Road bridge (A862). Conon Bridge village to left. Egress below bridge on right side (NH 143 559; 57.5549, -5.1080).

032 River Glass and River Beauly

Length	26km
OS	26
Grade	1/2

Distances
Some 26km for the main trip, a further 6km possible after a portage.

Portages
A portage of 2.5km will be required if the inaccessible part of the lower river is to be bypassed.

Introduction
This is a gem of a paddle from the Affric foothills, through lofty cliff amphitheatres with mixed woodland, forest and grassy farmland flats. This is Chisholm country, with the Clan seat at Cromar near the start of the paddle, and their eventual base at Erchlass Castle lower down near Struy. Wildlife abounds, eagles are often seen above, and otters, mink and pine martens.

Narrow passage, Aigas Gorge   © *Mary Connacher*

Itineraries
The river divides neatly into two separate days:
1. Fasnakyle to Mauld.
2. Mauld to Aigas.

Water level
The latter half of the trip will always be possible, due to the river becoming a reservoir behind the Aigas Dam, otherwise inspect the upper river from the bridge at Cannich.

Access
From the A831, which runs by the side of the river up to Cannich Bridge (NH 346 314; 57.3430, -4.7518), and the minor Glen Affric road, leaving it at the Fasnakyle Power Station (NH 321 294; 57.3241, -4.7920). The egress is at the Aigas Dam (NH 473 436; 57.4569, -4.5483),
To bypass the dam and paddle the lower section of the river access again at Kiltarlilty Bridge (NH 498 440; 57.4613, -4.5068), and final egress at Lovat Bridge (NH 515 450; 57.4709, -4.4791).

Campsites & accommodation
Campsite and Youth Hostel at Cannich. Cannich and Tomich have B&Bs, and good meals at Tomich Hotel, Slaters Arms, Cannich, and Cnoc and Glass restaurants in Struy.

Below Mauld Bridge, River Glass 📷 *Eddie Palmer*

Description

The river is grade 1, 2 on some corners, with trees down in places. It is popular with open canoeists, probably because it offers an intrepid-feeling trip, but is not remote at all. There is a strenuous carry out in the Aigas Gorge egress. The river usually has a dam release of about a foot on weekdays, in order to generate power, commencing very helpfully at about 9.00 a.m.

Km

0   Fasnakyle Power Station – parking on broad road verges, below power station. Fast section, good fun.

3   Cannich village, steep and bouldery access/egress at bridge.

3.5   River Cannich joins left. River becomes broad with tree-covered islands, and sandbanks. Lots of nice stopping places, long bends.

6.5   Eskadale. Access down a short track, estate road, from B-road on right bank, grassy river bank. After this point, the river becomes faster, with trees in the water. Care needed.

7.5   River winds near road on left bank, the main A831. Some parking places on side of road.

14.5 Mauld Bridge – Struy to the left. Easy access.

15   River Farrar joins from left, and the access from Struy bridge on the Farrar (0.5km upstream) is quite popular, but parking is very restricted. Turbulence where the Farrar joins.

23   Eilean Aigas island. By this time, the paddler will have already entered what is in fact a flat reservoir, (about 2km upstream) but not like one you have seen before! The island should be taken on the left side, but it can be circumnavigated, as there is no current. In low water, slight step in middle of gorge. On the right side is a fantastic road bridge access to the island, worth seeing. This is the Aigas Gorge, said to have one of the most Wow! factors of any open canoe trip in Scotland. As a household lives in the castle on the island, please respect their privacy. Landing is OK, but no litter, camping or fires please.

The section below the island often has otters present, and ospreys are commonly seen fishing here.

26   Aigas Power Station and dam. The egress is via a grass track on left side, before the dam, which leads up to a short tarmac road to the dam, from a car park.

Egress or Portage / Shuttle – There is another dam 2km downstream at Kilmorack, and no physical access. However, for those wishing to continue, the bridge just below Kilmorack offers access. (It appears that the River Glass becomes the Beauly below this point.)

28.5 Kiltarlilty Bridge. Parking and access on south (right) side. Many fishermen here in good water conditions.

29.5 Cruives Weir, long sloping weir.

34.5 Lovat Bridge, egress on right side, above

bridge. River becomes tidal, no further easy access, apart from perhaps a muddy exit at the back of Beauly village on the left bank.

033 Loch Monar

Length   Up to 26km round trip
OS   25

Introduction
Loch Monar has the unfortunate distinction of possessing a metalled road which is gated and locked at night-time. It is a rather bare landscape, with Munros all around it.

Access
The road and the area is owned by the local estate, but run by Scottish Nature as a nature reserve. The road runs for 22km up Glen Strathfarrar from Struy Bridge (NH 402 404; 57.4258, -4.6646) to the dam (NH 203 393; 57.4085, -4.9954).

Campsites & accommodation
There is a formal site at Cannich, or discreet wild camping.

Description
The landscape is rough and barren, the loch as a reservoir having the usual rocky sides in low water. It is 13km long. At least the paddler will see few if any people!

034 Loch Monar West to the Sea

Length   36km
OS   25/33
Grade   1/2/3 (some waterfalls).

Portages
There will probably be seven portages. Four 'uphill' portages, one of 1km, another of 0.5 km, and 3 'downhill', avoiding rapids and waterfalls.

Introduction
This is a creative route, only done by a very few people to the author's knowledge (and by kayak). It is very remote and serious, in that it has both rapids and waterfalls on the descent to the sea. Loch Monar is the 'private' and gated access road loch which can be frustrating to paddlers wishing for a longer expedition.
The route reaches the west coast at Loch Long, which runs off Loch Alsh.

Water level
The river sections need to be done after wet weather.

Access
From Loch Monar, as in Route 033.

Campsites & accommodation
Wilderness route, with wild camping.

Description
Paddle along Loch Monar west for 9km to Pait Lodge on the south side in an obvious bay. The route then goes 'uphill' via a short river to An Gead Loch, Loch an Tachdaich, a short burn up to Lochan Gobhlach, and a very short burn to another upper lochan.
This 6km, of not very high gradient, will have brought you to the east/west watershed, at a very obvious and wet bog. The headwaters of the River Ling are only 0.5km to the south-west. An initial 1.5km of the Allt an Loin-fhioda starts a westerly descent, to Loch

Loch Mullardoch   📷 *Mike Forrester*

Cruoshie, then 3.5km of flat river, followed by 2.5km of rapids down to the junction with the Blackwater, forming the River Ling.

The river falls rapidly over the next 3km until it is joined by a large burn from the south-east. The Ling then slows down and flattens for 5km until it enters a final gorge containing two large waterfalls. There is a footpath on the right bank here, and a 4x4 road high on the left bank. After 2km of gorge, a very final 1km leads into Loch Long, and a road of 9km down to Dornie.

Other important points
The route is 36km long, and takes 2–3 days.

035 Loch Mullardoch

Length   26km round trip
OS   25

Introduction
Loch Mullardoch is a long reservoir, which has banks that dry out in low water.

Access
Here at least the road is public, the minor road following the River Cannich up from the A831 in Strathglass (NH 338 319; 57.3472, -4.7655) to the dam (NH 220 317; 57.3410, -4.9615).

Campsites & accommodation
The nearest formal camping or accommodation is at Cannich. The area of the loch is wilderness.

Description
The loch is a 13km long reservoir, and Munros dominate to both north and south.

036 Loch Affric and Loch Beinn a Mheadhoin

Length   30km round trip
OS   25

Introduction
Glen Affric is worth visiting in its own right, it is the site of one of Scotland's greatest forest regeneration schemes, but it also offers two lochs set in beautiful scenery.

Access
The road runs up Strathglass from Inverness to Cannich, and then a minor road heads up the glen to a dead end near the top end of Loch Beinn a Mheadhoin at a parking place (NH 216 242; 57.2735, -4.9628).

Campsites & accommodation
Cannich.

Loch Beinn a Mheadhoin   📷 *Eddie Palmer*

Description

Loch Beinn a Mheadhoin can be accessed from near the dam, where the River Affric leaves. The loch is 9km long, heavily wooded, with inlets and islands. At the top of this loch is a short 'uphill' to Loch Affric, a 100m river. A further 6km will bring you to the top of the loch, in one of Scotland's great wildernesses, famous with climbers and walkers.

Short easy trip

Loch Beinn a Mheadhoin – round trip of 9km.

River Moriston 📷 *Mary Connachar*

037 River Moriston

Length	14km
OS	34
Grade	1/2

Introduction

A tranquil, lovely river, not often paddled, either because the glen is a bit further to travel to, or because of its association with the white water stretch below Dundreggan Reservoir, which flows into Loch Ness at Invermoriston.

Water level

The level is easy to judge at the put-in, below which are some easy grade 1 rapids – too rocky and 'scrapey', and the river is too low. In flood, the river is a more serious proposition.

Access

Glen Moriston is the route of Bonnie Prince Charlie's flight to Glen Elg and Skye. The put in, at Mackenzie's grave, is where Roderick Mackenzie is said to have deliberately sacrificed himself to the Redcoats, as a 'doppleganger', or substitute, in order to give the real prince time to escape. A roadside cairn, consecrated grave and memorial mark the spot, and this is about 3km down the river on the A887 (NH 237 112; 57.1577, -4.9187), the main east-west road, from its junction with the A87 from Invergarry.

Egress is on the left side, well before the dam, (NH 351 154; 57.1996, -4.7328), just where the forestry meets the main road, and an Armco barrier finishes. An old track runs up to the road. After this, the sides become steeper and rocky.

Campsites & accommodation

The nearest proper campsites are down on Loch Ness side, or at Fort Augustus. Invermoriston village has B&Bs, a restaurant and a hotel. In the summer at the village hall, as in many Highland communities, there are light lunches, and toilets available.

Description

The glen is broad and well-farmed, with virtually no habitation on the river, and very much quieter than the trunk road above would suggest. Ospreys are seen in the glen, at this their northern margin of range in Scotland.

Km

0   Mackenzie's Grave. Lay-by and steps down. Good current, eddy upstream. Islands, wooded banks, and plenty of stopping places.

River Ness 📷 *Greg Davies*

9   Torgoyle Bridge, main road passes over. Bridge built by Thomas Telford in 1808, swept away by a flood in 1818, and re-built in 1828. Almost identical design to Telford's bridge over the Tay at Dunkeld.

11   River becomes bouldery and braided, faster water.

12.5 River slows down as it imperceptibly becomes the reservoir behind Dundreggan Dam.

14   Egress is on the left side, well before the dam (NH 351 154; 57.1996, -4.7328), just where the forestry meets the main road, and an Armco barrier finishes. An old track runs up to the road. After this, the sides become steeper and rocky.

038 Loch Ness and River Ness

Length	7km, 13km or up to 38km
OS	26
Grade	1–2

Length
Loch Ness – up to 38km. River Ness – 7.5km to 13km.

Introduction
The Ness is the outlet for Loch Ness, and at some times of year flows fast and powerfully with a massive amount of water behind it. A trip from the top of the river also offers access to the north end of the loch, with endless kilometres of paddling. The river is pleasant and rural, considering the nearness of Inverness. Bird life is plentiful.

Water level
The River Ness is reached at Dochfour Weir, some rocks showing indicates a medium level. If covered, the river is high. If the rapids and weirs are a bit too much in flood, they can all be portaged.

Access
From Dochgarroch on the A82 south of Inverness (NH 618 405; 57.4337, -4.3047), giving access on to the Caledonian Canal, which can be paddled south to reach the river, or to go on Loch Ness. Egress at Bught Park in Inverness (NH 664 440; 57.4665, -4.2300).

Campsites & accommodation
Available at Dochgarroch.

Chatting with the lifeboat crew, Loch Ness   ⃝ *Eddie Palmer*

Short easy trip
Dochgarroch to Bught Park.

Description
For Loch Ness, see the Great Glen route in Section D, Cross-Scotland routes. To access Loch Ness from Dochgarroch, go 3km upstream through Loch Dochfour to Lochend.
River Ness
Km

0   Dochgarroch, 7km out of Inverness. Launch at/near the campsite, and paddle up the canal to reach the river at a weir. Dochfour Weir is the first weir, usually shot down main chute. If too low, boats can be carried over the face of the weir, which will be grassy. Islands, rapids, and waves.

2.5 Broken weir, with waves.

5.5 Holm Mills Weir. Keep left, and avoid the sluice gates. The weir can be safely shot, about two-thirds along its length down

an obvious chute. The new southern Inverness by-pass bridge then crosses overhead. Gentle rapids after this into Inverness.

7.5 Islands – Bught Park to left, parking and recommended egress (NH 664 440; 57.4665, -4.2300).

Downriver
It is possible to proceed downriver, but through the town, the river runs fast, with little easy egress, or parking for vehicles.

11.5 South Kessock on left bank – egress, but not good scenery.

13   North Kessock, on north side of Beauly Firth, with parking and egress (only recommended in calm weather).

Other important points
For more detailed information see *Great Glen Canoe Trail*, Donald Macpherson, Pesda Press, 978-1-906095-74-1.

Active Schools trip on the River Arkaig 📷 *Bridget Thomas*

West

Contents

Kyle of Lochalsh

Plockton, Loch Carron   🖾 *Eddie Palmer*

Kyle of Lochalsh

This area is the gateway to Skye, with many walking, climbing and canoeing opportunities; Lochalsh is the main village. The lochs to the north are fairly isolated, as is the Applecross peninsula.

039 Crowlin Islands

Length	6km
OS	24
Tides	Tidal streams weak

Tides and weather

Tidal streams run fastest in Caolas Mor, between the mainland and islands, and through Inner Sound – I knot at Springs. It is important to check for and avoid high winds.

Introduction

A trip across open sea to some interesting islands.

Access

These islands provide a nice little trip in very settled weather, from Toscaig at the very end of the public road (NG 710 378; 57.3729, -5.8152).

Campsites & accommodation

There is camping at Applecross, 7km north.

Description

The islands are 3km from the mainland, the last 1km being exposed. There are three islands, with 'The Harbour' being the very narrow strait between the two largest islands; fine for canoes and kayaks – the gap is filled with water at high tide. Eilean Mor, the largest island, was once inhabited and has ruined houses on the east side.

040 Loch Kishorn and Loch Carron

Length	Up to 46km round trip
OS	24
Tides	Tidal streams negligible

Introduction

These two connected lochs provide a paddle in fairly sheltered water, with magnificent mountain views. The main attraction in the area is Plockton village, of Hamish Macbeth TV fame, in Loch Carron.

Access

From Plockton (NG 80 34; 57.3432, -5.6619), at the end of a minor road from Kyle of Lochalsh; from Lochcarron (NG 89 39; 57.3923, -5.5165) on the A896 from Dingwall; and Ardaroch (NG 833 400; 57.3986, -5.6124), further west from Lochcarron on the A896.

Campsites & accommodation

Balmacara, just east of Kyle of Lochalsh.

Description

It is 3.5km between Kishorn Island at the mouth of Loch Kishorn, and Ardaroch village at its head. It's 4.5km from Kishorn Island over to Plockton village in Loch Carron. The route has islands and buoys, and Plockton is a very sheltered anchorage, and is very popular with yachtsmen in the summer. It's also very mild, with many palm trees. Travel E/NE for 15km to the very shallow and muddy head of the loch, passing the narrows at Stromeferry (former ferry point) and Lochcarron village, where the A896 road joins the loch. This is now in the heart of the Wester Ross mountains.

Short easy trip

Loch Carron – Plockton and harbour – this is a very sheltered round trip of 4km. Access from Plockton harbour at NG 79 33; 57.3338, -5.6777.

041 Loch Duich, Loch Alsh and Loch Long

Length	Up to 63km round trip
OS	33/25
Tides	See Introduction

Introduction

These three lochs stretch inland from Skye and the Kyle, and provide relatively safe paddling in mouth-watering scenery. The outer part of Loch Alsh has strong tidal streams, as sea water pours through Kyle Rhea to the south. The rest of the lochs have only weak tides.

Access

From the A87 along the north side of both Loch Duich and Loch Alsh.

Campsites & accommodation

Balmacara and Glenshiel.

Description

At Kyleakin, there is much ship traffic proceeding either north or south under the Skye Bridge (always a good photo opportunity), and passage east from here (NG 76 27; 57.2786, -5.7221) close to the north shore is advised. Camping can be found at Balmacara (NG 802 280; 57.2896, -5.6533), just 4km east of Lochalsh. The coast is low and rocky; 5km from Balmacara to Glas Eilean, then 3km on to Dornie village (shops, B&Bs etc).

Skye Bridge, Loch Alsh　　　　　　　　　　　　　　　　　📷 *Mike Hayward*

From here, Loch Long extends 11km to the north-east, in a very narrow and interesting fjord-like valley between mountains.

Also at Dornie is the famous Eilean Donan castle on its rock promontary, one of the most photographed castles in Scotland, if not Europe – well worth visiting. Loch Duich then runs south-east from this point 8.5km to Shiel Bridge, at the foot of Glenshiel (small campsite here).

Short easy trip

Dornie (NG 88 26; 57.2753, -5.5220) to Invershiel (NG 93 19; 57.2148, -5.4331) and return. This is a round trip of 16km but can be shortened at will.

042 Loch Duich to Loch Hourn

Length 52km

OS 33

Tides　　Strong tidal streams

Introduction

This trip is 38km from Shiel Bridge round to Arnisdale on Loch Hourn, and another 14km into Kinloch Hourn. The ideal trip is to take three days or so to enjoy the scenery and wildlife. Requires a period of settled weather. See also descriptions in Route 041.

Access

Shiel Bridge on A87 (NG 93 18; 57.2059, -5.4322), Arnisdale (NG 84 10; 57.1300, -5.5744) on Loch Hourn (minor road from Glenelg), and Kinloch Hourn (NG 06 95; 57.8475, -6.9674) at head of Loch Hourn, reached by a long single-track road from Invergarry on the Great Glen.

Campsites & accommodation

There is a formal site at Shiel Bridge and a bothy and campsite at Barrisdale Bay on Loch Hourn. There is also wild camping.

Description

The route is sheltered along the south shore of Lochs Duich and Alsh, but after rounding Garbhan Cosach, Kyle Rhea has very fast tidal streams, and accurate calculations are necessary. The ideal, no matter how many days are being taken, is to use the ebb tide to take you down Kyle Rhea (7 knots at spring tides!), and on to the area of the Sandaig Islands, or south of there. A flood can then propel you up Loch Hourn. Past the Kyle Rhea ferry is Glenelg, a useful stopping point, with village shop and pub. Sandaig is *Ring of Bright Water* country, where the book was written, and where otters are frequently seen.

The map or chart will tell the paddler that the 4km from Sandaig to Glas Eilean are exposed., and it is 5km from here to the safety and shelter of Arnisdale. Wild campsites are frequent, and of high quality.

For detailed description of the end of the trip, see Route 043 Loch Hourn.

Steve Green   *Bob Hamilton*

043 Loch Hourn

Length	Round trip of up to 27km
OS	33
Tides	Strong tidal streams in narrows

Introduction

Loch Hourn is one of the magnificent west coast fjords giving access to Knoydart, and well worth a trip in its own right.

Access

At the head of Loch Hourn is Kinlochhourn (NG 06 95; 57.8475, -6.9674), now with a reasonable car park, where vehicles may be left for days. The access road from Glen Garry and Glen Quoich is very narrow and steep, with many awkward corners. There are no other roads out to Knoydart, only a track for walkers to Barrisdale Bay (NG 86 04; 57.0771, -5.5362).

Campsites & accommodation

Plenty of wild camping out on Knoydart, with a bothy and campsite at Barrisdale Bay.

Description

The first part out into the loch is narrow, with swift tides, and after 5.5km the narrows at Caolas Mor is reached. Progress will not be made against the tide here. A further 2km brings you round to the beautiful Barrisdale Bay to the left (south), which offers a campsite at Barrisdale Farm, and access to the Knoydart mountains. The most sensible plan is to calculate to arrive at the narrows just before high tide, and in the bay at high tide, to avoid a long portage ashore.

A 6km paddle further out to the north shore reaches Arnisdale, from where a ferry runs to Barrisdale in the summer. A further 5km brings one to the headland on the south side, but there is a lot of exposure here.

Mallaig

Loch Morar to Loch Nevis portage *Bob Hamilton*

Mallaig

Mallaig is the major ferry and fishing port on the west central coast, at the end of a long road from Fort William. It is more a working town than a resort like Oban, but it has many attractions nearby and gives access to Skye, via the Armadale car ferry, and the Small Isles. Loch Nevis is included in this section, although it can only be reached by sea.

044 Loch Nevis

Length	28km
OS	40
Tides	Tidal streams negligible

Distances
Trip of 28km from Inverie, to head of loch, and back to Inverie.

Introduction
Loch Nevis can either be reached (if you have an inflatable or folding craft) by foot ferry

from Mallaig to Inverie, or by a bit of an expedition. Both the sea route and the route by portage over from Loch Morar are covered in Route 046. It is a fabulous sea loch surrounded by mountains, and well-known for very strong local winds coming down from the mountains.

045 Loch Morar

Length	Round trip of up to 36km
OS	40

Introduction
A lovely west-coast loch, separated from the sea by the sands of the very short River Morar, and the main road to Mallaig. It is obviously more sheltered than the sea lochs to the north.

Access
Loch Morar is easily accessed from Mallaig and Arisaig, via a minor road leading off the A830 to a pier alongside the first part of the loch

Fun with Active Schools, Loch Morar   📷 *B. Thomas*

(NM 689 929; 56.9694, -5.8084), and eventually to the hamlet of Bracorina.

Campsites & accommodation

The nearest formal sites are just south towards Arisaig (six sites at the last count on this lovely stretch of coast, some of which may only take caravans). There are plenty of wild sites along Loch Morar.

Description

There are attractive wooded islands in the first few kilometres, and the loch stretches some 18km to the east, being a uniform 2km wide, narrowing to 1km. After 10km paddling east, there is a pier on the south side giving access to an estate, and after 11km, on the north side is the landing and portage at Swordland (or just round the corner at South Tarbet bay, where a track leads over to Loch Nevis at Tarbet. See Route 046). A further 7km to the end of the loch leads to Glen Pean and Glen Dessary, great walking country.

Short easy trip

From Bracorina or pier at NM 689 929; 56.9694, -5.8084 out to the islands and back – 4km.

046 Loch Morar and Loch Nevis

Length	26km or 40km
OS	33/40
Tides	Tidal streams negligible

Distances

Possible expeditions of 40km round trip, either using the route to reach Inverie, or the head of Loch Nevis. Round trip of 26km to reach Mallaig.

Portages

One portage of 2km over the tarbet (narrow neck of land) between the two lochs.

Introduction

A fine trip in great scenery, which can be quite safe if conditions are closely observed on Loch Nevis. A week's holiday can be spent in this area.

Access

From the pier on Loch Morar (NM 689 929; 56.9694, -5.8084).

Campsites & accommodation

Wild camping.

Description

The classic way into Loch Nevis is by Loch Morar, along to Swordland, and then over the portage to Tarbet, a not too rough way (track with stones) over the pass, just under 2km.

On the north side is a chapel converted into a bothy, and camping available. There are two great directions to go now: east, up Loch Nevis to the head, 8km, or west 8km, out to Inverie, the 'capital village' of Knoydart, with its pub and lively social scene.

To do both will usually take four days, with start and return to the west end of Loch Morar. A different route, with more risk, is to return by sea to Mallaig, which is 9.5km. The safest way is to cross over (away from the ferry and fishing boat route) to the south shore off Sgeir a' Ghaill, sheltered from westerlies, and then hug the south shore, which is high and rocky. This trip is only about 2 hours max with the tide, so the risk is quite slight if prevailing weather is benign. Whichever way you go, this is a classic.

Loch Shiel   📷 *Bridget Thomas*

047 Loch Shiel

Length	Round trip of up to 60km
OS	40

Introduction

Loch Shiel is a wilderness experience, as there are no roads apart from at either end of the loch. It is 30km long from Glenfinnan, the famous monument on the 'Road to the Isles' at the north end, to Acharacle at the southern end. Wildlife is plentiful, with otters, pine martens, golden eagles, and if very lucky, wild cats.

Access

Access may be had at the north end, Glenfinnan, via the hotel (NM 901 805; 56.8683, -5.4489). At Acharacle, access/egress can be slightly difficult. A pier on the left (east) side at Acharacle is much used by commercial boats, and there is almost no parking. A better bet is to egress just after the bridge, entering the River Shiel on the left bank. All the roads in the area are narrow, with little parking.

There are so many visitors nowadays to the Glenfinnan viaduct, that extra vehicle parking is being developed.

Campsites & accommodation

Wild camping in many places down the loch. In summer, shingle spits are better to avoid midges. The site at Resipole on Loch Sunart is the nearest formal campsite.

Description

The scenery is superb all the way down. A day trip will only take the paddler halfway down and back, but camping can be had in many places. Small islands become much more frequent about halfway down. After 20km you come to the first large bay on the left, where the River Polloch comes in. Polloch village is 1km inland from the end of the inlet, with a road egress (a very tortuous road over from Strontian on Loch Sunart).

Some 2km further on at the narrows is the well-known Burial Ground Island, Eilean Fhianain, and St Firman's Chapel. The left bank then opens out into Claish Moss, a large bog, and Acharacle follows after a further 6km.

Short easy trips

Glenfinnan to Scamadale jetty (NM 83 73; 56.7978, -5.5591) and return, (20km); or Sheil Bridge to St Finnan's Island (burial ground), at NM 75 68 (16km return).

048 Loch Sheil to Loch Eilt

Loch Shiel, River Shiel, Loch Moidart, Loch Ailort and Loch Eilt

Length	70 or 110km
OS	40/41
Grade	1/2
Tides	Tidal streams weak

River Sheil 📷 *Jonny Hawkins*

Distances

Glenfinnan, start and finish, 70km. Fort William, start and finish, 110km.

Tides

There are weak tidal streams from the seaward end of Loch Moidart north up the coast up to entrance of Loch Ailort.

Grade

Grade 1 and 2, but the fall at the end of the River Shiel might be more difficult (subject to tide).

Portages

The Glenfinnan circuit has portages of 2.5km up the River Ailort, and 6km from Loch Eilt to Loch Shiel.

The Fort William circuit has, in addition to the two portages above, one of 6km between Loch Shiel and Loch Eil.

Introduction

This trip of four days or so duration is a Scottish classic, and has been extended to a longer expedition leaving Fort William, and using Loch Eil and its connecting rivers to Glenfinnan. It is popular because it is circular, one of few in Scotland using rivers and lochs, and because of the scenery of Loch Shiel and the coast.

Water Level

The River Shiel can be very shallow in summer, the height is obvious from Shiel Bridge, Acharacle.

Access

At Glenfinnan, hotel pier (NM 901 805; 56.8683, -5.4489), egress possible at Acharacle (southern end of Loch Shiel), A860 at Glenuig (NM 674 777; 56.8324, -5.8191), A861 alongside Loch Ailort (various places over 4km), Lochailort village (NM 768 824; 56.8791, -5.6690), and Glenfinnan.

Campsites & accommodation

There are plenty of wild camping sites. The nearest formal site is at Resipole, Loch Sunart (not on route).

Description

See Route 047 Loch Shiel, and Route 049 Loch Moidart. The River Shiel is only 3.5km long and at the bottom a sizeable rapid debouches you into the sea at low tide. The river is narrow all the way down, with fishing platforms and other detritus sticking out into the channel – no other obstacles. Leaving Moidart by North Channel, turn north for 5km of coast, with pleasant islands and inlets inside of

River Shiel exit rapid 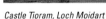 *Robert Craig*　*Castle Tioram, Loch Moidart* *Pete White*

Samalaman Island, to Glenuig, a very hospitable place, with a famous village hall offering great music all through the summer. Camping on the foreshore here.

It is 3.5km on to Roshven, and then a further 2km to islands, often used for camping. The scenery remains fine, and it is only 5km more to Lochailort village. Then a 2.5km portage to Loch Eilt, 5.5km long, and a 7km portage on to Glenfinnan (or leave a car at Lochailort!).

049 Loch Eilt

Length　Round trip of up to10km
OS　40

Loch Eilt is 5km long, and offers a short trip in mountain scenery. It is often subject to high winds from the west. Access is off the A 830 road on the north side. Paddling west to east there are small parking places, commencing at NM 79 82; 56.8766, -5.6325, and finishing at NM 83 81; 56.8695, -5.5659.

050 Loch Ailort

Length　Round trip of up to 12km
OS　40
Tides　Weak tidal steams in narrows

Introduction
This is an attractive sea loch, running south-west to north east, with the main A861 alongside the south shore. It is 6km long.

Access
The easiest access is from a parking place at NM 729 785; 56.8423, -5.7296. Other access/ egress points are at the head of the loch, near Lochailort itself, which is a tiny settlement, either on the large beach, or at a jetty or pier. Be careful not to impede local fishermen in this area.

Description
This is a lovely loch to explore. There are good wild camping sites on the headland and islands at the sea end of the loch, and also on islands in the narrows further up the loch.

051 Loch Moidart

Length　Round trip of up to 22km
OS　40
Tides　Tidal streams negligible

Introduction
Loch Moidart has sheltered water, great scenery, and a castle! There is also variety in that a number of different routes may

65

The Small Isles from Loch Moidart 📷 *Ben McKeown*

Loch Sunart 📷 *Steve Green*

be paddled. For walking or cycling, beach combing, or wild camping in quiet places, this is one of the best places in Scotland.

Access

The head at Ardmorlich pier on the A861 (NM 697 728; 56.7896, -5.7769) is often dry, and a more reliable way of finding water is to travel down to Castle Tioram (NM 663 724; 56.7843, -5.8323), a ruin reached down the road running alongside the River Shiel from Shiel Bridge. There is a car park at the end, much used by walkers, and people who come to stare at the castle, crumbling away due to arguments between its owner and the conservation authorities.

Campsites & accommodation

There are great campsites all over this area, especially on the islands. Please camp well away from houses.

Description

Launching will always be possible at Castle Tioram (pronounced 'Churram'), and the paddler has then the glories of Shona Beag and Eilean Shona islands, as well as a couple of smaller islands to paddle around (14km for the round trip).

If you are feeling brave and the weather is settled, there is a little expedition to the south well worth carrying out. Go out of South Channel, and turn left at Farquhar's Point, some 2.5km round to Ardtoe (NM 628 708; 56.7682, -5.8882), a delightful spot with beautiful sandy beaches. Inland from here is Kentra, an interesting area of little creeks, if there is water. Then 2.5km further south-west from Ardtoe is Gortenfern (NM 612 691; 56.7522, -5.9128), with another fabulous beach, also reached by a walk from Arivegaig.

Short easy paddle

From Castle Tioram to Eilean Shona and return – 2km

052 Loch Sunart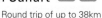

Length	Round trip of up to 38km
OS	40/49
Tides	Tidal streams are weak

Introduction

Loch Sunart is another fabulous area, easily providing a week's holiday with different trips each day. A base at, say, Resipole campsite just before Salen gives access to beaches on Ardnamurchan, the whole of the main loch, Loch Shiel to the north, and Loch Teacuis on

West entrance to Loch Teacuis 📷 *Tony Hammock*

the south side, an area few people are privileged to see, especially by water.

Access

The north side has a road all the way along it, the A861 as far as Salen, and then the B8007 which eventually winds its way to Ardnamurchan Point. Access may be had at Strontian (NM 815 615; 56.6940, -5.5738), Resipole Farm and landing (NM 725 640; 56.7121, -5.7232), Salen (NM 690 648; 56.7175, -5.7812), a useful picnic and car park near the west (NM 680 630; 56.7009, -5.7959) and, with some difficulty, near the Glenborrodale Hotel (NM 620 606; 56.6764, -5.8918). However all of the roads are narrow, mostly single-track, and can be extremely congested in summer. Care is especially required with trailers.

Campsites & accommodation

Resipole campsite is well-situated, with space for tents, caravans, and camper vans, and it has cabins for rent, as well as a bar and restaurant. There is no other site in the area.

Description

Due to the normal prevailing tide and wind further out in the loch, it is advised to access from the Ardnamurchan road, around Glen-

borrodale, north side (actually little parking in this area, the hotel just east of Glenborrodale has a jetty and will probably oblige).

Isle of Risga lies just off here, and a passage east, using the shelter provided by it, can mean a crossing over to Carna, west side if the weather is fair, and entering Loch Teacuis through the very narrow western passage. The tide runs very fast here, enter preferably near the top of flood. The loch is 5km long, and very wild and isolated. There are campsites, but also terrible midges in summer. The east passage is wider, but with two rock reefs, an interesting paddle or sail.

Carna to Salen village, 9km. There is a picnic site on the left bank, just before Salen, which is extremely convenient for launching. Resipole campsite is 3.5km further on. The Ben Resipole path leaves from the campsite.

Opposite Resipole are some small islets, lots of seals.

Resipole to the 'Narrows', Glas Eilean, 5km. Nice islands on left side, habitat for otters. The narrow part has, as you would expect, strong tidal streams.

Glas Eilean to Strontian village, 6km. At low tide, much mud and sand off Strontian. There is a jetty 1km further on which is easier, with parking. Strontian is the main centre up at this part of the loch, but don't expect supermarkets!

The parking of vehicles is difficult in the whole of this area; the roads are narrow with 'passing places only' in most parts.

Short easy trip

Resipole campsite to the narrows and back – 10km

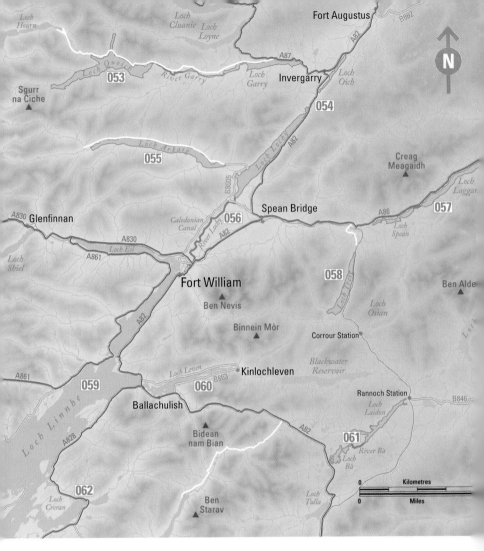

Fort William

Camping on the Upper River Garry   📷 *Pete White*

Fort William

Fort William is a famous and obvious centre for outdoor activities in Scotland. It has high mountains, including Ben Nevis, but as one of the wettest places in the UK is also probably the Scottish centre for white-water paddling. There are some wet-weather attractions in the town, plus supermarkets and outdoor shops. It is the start of the Great Glen route, has the rail route to Mallaig and the Isles, and plenty of accommodation to suit all tastes. The road north-east to Inverness has plenty of canoeing attractions off it.

053 Loch Quoich, Upper River Garry and Loch Garry 🛶 🌊 🐾

Length	Up to 46km
OS	33/34
Grade	1/2/3

Introduction

This route is included as a single trip, but is difficult in parts, especially for open canoes. Escape is always possible on the road to the north. The area has little habitation and lovely unspoilt rivers and lochs. Many climbers and walkers use Loch Quoich to gain access to the many Munros to the south and west. It can give a good three days' paddling.

Access

Access is via the A87 to Skye, turning off on the B-road (single track) to Kinloch Hourn alongside Loch Garry. It is then a drive of about 20 miles, taking an hour to reach the point where the road starts to leave Loch Quoich NM 989 036; 56.1825, -5.2447). Access should be had wherever the road is near the water. From the bridge over an arm of the loch, (NN 015 040; 56.1871, -5.2030), it is 10km to the head of the loch, in a mountain fastness. Egress near Garry dam (NN 069 023; 56.1741, -5.1147).

Campsites & accommodation
Wild camping. The site at the western end of the loch, surrounded by high mountains, is unforgettable.

Description
From the head of the loch, east to the dam is 14km, with a carry over the dam via the road. It is 3km with rapids on the Gearr Garry to the junction with the River Kingie. The river can often be either too low, and very rocky, or in flood when it is dangerous. Inspect first. At the junction, the river is far bigger and flows around wooded islands into Loch Poulary, which then becomes the River Garry, and into Loch Garry 8km downstream. There is one large rapid around islands on this stretch. Great campsites on some of the islands.
Loch Garry is 11km long, passing under an estate bridge at the narrows, a third of the way down. Egress is on to a track on left side, just before the dam. Below the dam is the white-water Garry (See *Scottish White Water*).

054 Loch Oich and Loch Lochy

Length	Up to 23.5km
OS	34

Upper River Garry   🖸 *Pete White*

Loch Quoich   🖸 *Liam McKeown*

Distances
Loch Lochy 15km, Canal is 2.5km, and Loch Oich 6km.

Portages
Portage at Laggan Locks at north end of Loch Lochy.

Introduction
These two lochs provide useful day trips in great scenery, Loch Lochy being the first experience many paddlers have of Canadian-like lake scenery.

Access
Road access to both lochs is from the main A82 road which runs up the glen, many parking places on east side of Loch Lochy (NN 25 91; 56.9770, -4.8830 to NN 27 94; 57.0046, -4.8522), fewer on Loch Oich, though there is one picnic site on west bank (NN 304 989; 57.0499, -4.7994).

Campsites & accommodation
Wilderness sites on west side of Loch Lochy, and possibly near mouth of River Garry, west side of Loch Oich.

Loch Arkaig   📷 *Carol Pudsey*

Description
Full details in the Cross-Scotland section, Route D Great Glen, Fort William to Inverness. Lochy is large, Oich is small and cosy, with interesting wooded islands.

Short easy trip
Loch Oich – from the picnic site on the west bank (NN 304 989; 57.0499, -4.7994) paddle around the loch and back – 6km.

055 Loch Arkaig

Length	Round trip of up to 38km
OS	33/34

Introduction
Loch Arkaig is an enormous and hidden loch, usually found by paddlers doing the very short River Arkaig. The very long and tedious lochside road gives access to the mountains of Glen Dessary at the west end.

Access
The B8005 leaves the Caledonian Canal at Gairlochy, 5km from Spean Bridge, crosses the outlet of the River Arkaig, winds through woodland, and emerges at the bottom end of Loch Arkaig. Parking is very restricted, there being a spot by the waterfalls 0.5km from the

east end of the loch, (NN 176 889; 56.9553, -5.0033) and some space right on the loch at its foot (NN 172 888; 56.9542, -5.0098).

Campsites & accommodation
The only spaces for wild camping appear to be right at the west end of the road alongside the loch.

Description
There is no habitation to speak of and the loch is 19km long, an almost uniform 1km wide. The upper reaches are amongst one of the wildest parts of Scotland, Knoydart lying to the west of here.

Other important points
The braver might want to paddle the river out, which is quite easy apart from the one grade 4 rapid (see *Scottish White Water*). The very short 2km river spits out the paddler very suddenly, onto the stillness of Loch Lochy at Bunarkaig, with a 4km trip south to either Gairlochy lock on the canal, or onto the River Lochy.

056 River Lochy

Length	11.5km
OS	41
Grade	1(2-3)

Grade
Grade 1, apart from Torcastle Rapid, grade 2/3, which can be portaged on the right-hand side over rocks.

Introduction
This rather attractive river is the extension of the Spean from Mucomir power station, and offers a pleasant paddle down towards Fort William, with one rapid which has provided

Torcastle Rapid, River Lochy   📷 *Pete White*

River Lochy   📷 *Bridget Thomas*

much trouble to the unwary. It is a flat grade 1, apart from Torcastle Rapid (Eas nan Long, 'Waterfall of the Ship'), which is graded 2/3.

Water Level
The first shingle rapids downstream of the start are a good indication of level.

Access
From the B8004, after it passes Mucomir power station, north-west of Spean Bridge (NN 183 839; 56.9107, -4.9882). Egress on to left bank, just above outflow from Fort William smelter, just before railway bridge (NN 119 755; 56.8328, -5.0872). To reach this by road, drive towards Fort William on the A82, and half a mile after the traffic lights at A830 junction, turn right on to minor road signed Inverlochy Castle. Take first right, then left and park just through the railway bridge.

Campsites & accommodation
Torness, near the start, Spean Bridge, or Glen Nevis.

Description
Km
0   Access near Gairlochy, where road leaves the river.

4   River Loy (see *Scottish White Water*) joins on right. It is worth a walk to see where the Loy flows under the Caledonian Canal aqueduct, and it can be paddled with water.

7   Torcastle Rapid is heralded by the river flowing left through a gap, and a change to a rocky river bed. The river drops between rock walls. In low water, it is a drop on the right into a pool; in high flows, the water is more confused and boily. Many capsizes here! Rescue however is easy, as is taking photos from the right bank (inspect/portage on right bank). Rocks and trees in water follow. River then slows down and meanders.

9.5   On a long, long left-hand bend, egress is possible on to right bank, just after houses.

11   Main road bridge, Fort William to Mallaig road.

11.5 Railway bridge and then egress should be made before it on to a lane from the main road. At the egress is also the outflow from aluminium works, which can offer sport to headbangers and is best avoided.

Loch Laggan in high winds   📷 Greg Davies

Loch Treig   📷 Steve Green

057 Loch Laggan and Loch Spean

Length	17km
OS	41/42

Introduction
These two lochs are linked, and often regarded as one piece of water. They are reservoirs and can be quite empty in dry periods.

Access
Access can be had at the eastern end at Kinloch Laggan, on the River Pattack, off the A86, main east-west road (NN 538 898; 56.9762, -4.4081). Access/egress also from where the river coming down the Creag Meagaidh corrie joins the loch, where there is also a good car park (NN 481 870; 56.9492, -4.5003). Final egress off at the dam (NN 371 809; 56.8908, -4.6773) where there is some parking.

Campsites & accommodation
Roybridge, Inverroy and Spean Bridge. Bunkhouse at Roybridge.

Description
From the attractive sandy beach at the eastern end (when the water in the reservoir is low)

it is 11km to the western end. Ardverikie Castle is very obvious on the south side after a few kilometres, and Munros dominate to both north and south. Halfway down on the north side is the car park for Creag Meagaidh, a good stopping point, and adequate car parking.

At the end of Loch Laggan there is a small barrage to portage around.

The Spean between the two lochs is hardly visible or flowing in high water, when there is in effect one continuous loch. Loch Spean is much smaller and narrower, and visibility is limited to the immediate surroundings due to islands of mud when low. The loch is 5.5km long, with take-out on the north side by the Laggan Dam. If lucky, you might see pipes 'blowing' from this dam, a great sight indeed. It is interesting to go and look at the horrendous gorges lower down the Spean.

058 Loch Treig

Length	Round trip of 18km
OS	41

Introduction
Loch Treig is in a very spectacular position, and usually only seen by passengers on the train from Glasgow. It is a reservoir, part of the Glen

Loch Linnhe   [📷] *Sue Tadman*

Spean system, lying south of the main glen, in the Grey Corries set of mountains.

Access
Road access is from the minor road to Fersit (NN 353 781; 56.8650, -4.7050) off the A86, and at which end is car parking.

Campsites & accommodation
At Spean Bridge, Inverroy and Roybridge. Bunkhouse at Roybridge.

Description
The loch is 9km long, situated amongst high and wild mountains. There is a hunting lodge at the bottom end, reached only from Corrour Station.

059 Loch Linnhe

Length	50km
OS	41/49
Tides	Tidal streams strong in narrows

Distances
Loch Linnhe runs for 50km from Oban north-east to Fort William.

Tides
Tidal streams are generally weak, but they do strengthen at locations of narrows, noticeably at Corran narrows and ferry point, the entrance to Loch Leven under Ballachulish Bridge, and around the north end of Lismore, and Shuna.

Introduction
Loch Linnhe is large and exposed, but a couple of arms off it are included below. It is the main approach for shipping heading for the Caledonian Canal.

Access
From Oban, Port Appin, Corran and Fort William on the east side. The west side is much more remote, although the road north from Ardgour, on the west side of the Corran Ferry, is pretty and quieter than the east side.

Campsites & accommodation
Sites and accommodation at Oban, Fort William, Glencoe and Ballachulish.

Description
North of Oban is the entrance to Loch Etive,

Eilean Munde, Loch Leven 📷 *Tony Hammock*

and then the narrowing of the Lynn of Lorne towards Appin. This area is interesting, with narrows and islands between Port of Appin and Lismore. Around the north side of Lismore are shallows and islands off Port Ramsay. North of this is Shuna, narrow passage to east, and then the headland between Cuil and Kentallan, good camping possibilities.

Around this corner is the entrance east into Loch Leven and Ballachulish, and then to the north the Corran Narrows, very strong tides, and ferry.

The way up to Fort William is much more sheltered from the wind. At the very top is Corpach, and the entrance to the Caledonian Canal. To the left (west), is Loch Eil.

060 Loch Leven

Length	Up to 26km
OS	41/49
Tides	Strong in area of narrows

Tides
Tidal streams are strong under Ballachulish Bridge, and the islands just inland from here. Otherwise weak.

Introduction
Loch Leven often provides a safe and sheltered sea paddle when it is windy elsewhere, with good mountain scenery all the way up to Kinlochleven.

Access
There is a launching ramp just after the Ballachulish Bridge (NN 054 598; 56.6893, -5.1818), reached by a minor road from North Ballachulish. The end of the loch at Kinlochleven is very dry at low tide, but there are several places to egress on the north shore on to small vehicle parking places.

Campsites & accommodation
At Kinlochleven, Caolasnacon on the south bank, and in Glen Coe on the south shore.

Description
It is 13km up to Kinlochleven, a nice half-day paddle, with the scenery of Glen Coe ever-present. There are various access places on both banks where the trip could be shortened. After 3km paddling east you come to the island of Eilean Munde, the burial place of the Lords of the Isles. At 5km the loch narrows,

Loch Bá, Rannoch Moor 📷 *Eddie Palmer*

Garbh Ghaoir, Rannoch Moor 📷 *Jonny Hawkins*

and at 8.5km are real narrows. It is advisable to reach the head of the loch at high tide, the drying out part being boulders and seaweed.

Short easy trip

Ballachulish Bridge inland to Glencoe village and return – 10km.

061 Rannoch Moor

Lochs Bà and Laidon, Rannoch Station

Length	13km
OS	41/50/42
Grade	1

Portages

In low water and dry summers, the first part of the trip could entail some short portages.

Introduction

This is another classic trip, Rannoch Moor is never forgotten by anybody who has crossed it, and many forms of transport have been tried, canoe, kayak, lilo, raft, etc.

Access

The start is at one of Britain's most remote and windswept points, as the A82 crosses over

to Glen Coe. This comes into the expedition category because high summer brings low water, lots of mud and many midges, other seasons often unseasonable snow and sleet showers. Once on the moor, there is literally no escape, it's either onwards ... or back. The vehicle shuttle for this is also massive – almost across Scotland! - about 83 miles one-way to Rannoch Station!

The start is on east side of Loch Bà, where a small connecting river flows under the road, the only bridge on this road. It is just after a large lochan on the west side (NN 309 495; 56.6068, -4.7583). Beware, there is only one lay-by to park in on this bit of road.

Egress is off the Dubh Lochan, north side (NN 417 578; 56.6851, -4.5874) after Loch Laidon.

Campsites & accommodation

On the route, look for slightly higher ground – everywhere is boggy. No formal sites nearby, apart from down in Glen Coe.

Description

The scenery is very flat, albeit surrounded by mountains, and navigation is therefore quite difficult - a GPS comes into its own in this terrain. Loch Bà is some 2.5km long, and heads generally north-east, but has islands, and is

Loch Creran   📷 *Tony Hammock*

062 Loch Creran Ⓢ

Length	12.5km
OS	49
Tides	Tidal streams negligible within loch

Tides
Tidal streams are negligible within the loch but the entrance from the sea has very fast tidal streams, being bottle-shaped.

quite misleading. There are two places where the loch narrows, the second one heralding a turn of the loch to the right, and the start of the River Bà. The river is often imperceptible in its flow so not obvious, and in certain levels of water, dead-end channels can mislead paddlers.

The river winds for 2.5km eventually into Loch Laidon, which is obvious! The intrepid voyageur can now perhaps relax a bit, and enjoy the surrounding scenery. The trip should take more than a day to appreciate this piece of wilderness, and the first more comfortable campsites are on the tiny wooded islands in Loch Laidon. This loch is 8km long, with a long arm out to the north-west into yet more wilderness. The route ahead is framed by the mountains of the Rannoch deer forest to the north.

At the end of Loch Laidon (carefully avoiding the outlet of the Garbh Ghaoir river), is a short half km portage from the little Dubh Lochan up a track to Rannoch Station.

Introduction
This is another arm off Loch Linnhe, not incredibly interesting but the upper loch, now above the road bridge, is quiet.

Access
From the A828, Oban to Fort William road, on the south side of the Creagan Bridge (NM 976 442; 56.5461, -5.2970), or from the minor road to South Shian jetty (NM 976 442; 56.5461, -5.2970), off the A828 near Benderloch.

Campsites & accommodation
Ledaig, south of Benderloch, or nearer to Oban.

Description
Eriska, at the mouth, is a separate island at low tide with a hotel on it. South Shian has a major boatyard and yacht moorings. 10km from the entrance to the A828 bridge, and a further 2.5km to the end.

Short easy paddle
A paddle of some 5km round trip on the upper loch from the road bridge (NM 976 442; 56.5461, -5.2970).

Oban

Stunning day on Loch Etive   📷 *Stuart Wagstaff*

Oban

Most visitors to the West Highlands will at some time or other have been through Oban. It is the largest town on the coast, and a major ferry port, the gateway to most of the Inner Hebrides, and to Barra in the Outer Hebrides. It is bustling in the summer months, and has every facility.

063 Loch Etive

Length	Round Trip of up to 54km
OS	49/50
Tides	Fast tidal streams in narrows

Tides

This loch is famous for the tidal rapid under Connel Bridge, the 'Falls of Lora', which run at 7 knots plus at springs. Inland from here, the only real tidal effect is at the narrows at Bonawe, giving strong tide at springs.

The Falls of Lora (which can be avoided by staying close to south shore) provide rough water at certain states of tide.

Introduction

Just to the north of Oban is the entrance to Loch Etive, a long tidal loch with many features and points of interest. It is mainly known as a loch to paddle from the head at Glen Etive, amongst the Glen Coe mountains, or for the honey pot of the tidal Falls of Lora, not far from the entrance and still unusual enough to draw many tourists.

Access

Dunstaffnage Bay, east of Oban (NM 885 340; 56.4506, -5.4369); Connel, north bank (NM 909 346; 56.4570, -5.3984); Achnacoich pier (NM 961 340; 56.4539, -5.3134); Airds Bay jetty, end of River Awe / Bonawe narrows (NN 011 327; 56.4444, -5.2312); and head of loch from Glen Etive (NN 108 450; 56.5587, -5.0827).

Campsites & accommodation

Ledaig, north of Connel; wild camping sites on sides of upper loch.

Description

In sheltered weather, it is possible to paddle up from Oban. From the entrance at Eilean Mor, immediately to south (right) is Dunstaffnage Marina, the largest on the coast now, and after 2km are the Falls of Lora, under Connel Bridge, which run very strongly on a spring ebb tide. The main passage for boats is close to the right (south) bank. The left has a rock ledge which uncovers, and if an ebb tide, there are bound to be small white-water kayaks playing on it. For an easy passage, go up on the flood.

At 4km, Achnacoich River, fish farms from here on up.

7km, Airds Point. 10km, Bonawe Narrows.

It is a further 17km up to the head, with only mountains, mountains, mountains! Plenty of possible campsites. In the height of summer, the head of the loch can be quite crowded with people camping, so maybe use the advantage of being on the water to avoid this area.

Short easy trip

Bonawe narrows to Inverliver Bay and return – 13km, towards head of loch – up to 34km round trip is possible.

064 Lower Orchy

Length	12.5km
OS	50/55
Grade	1/2 (3)

Portages

You may choose to portage the weir and the portage around the rapids is about 600m long.

Introduction

The Orchy is of course far better known as a white-water river, but there is a pleasant stretch where the river flattens out in the lower valley, downstream of the third and final waterfall. There is, however, a stretch of grade 3 rocky rapids in the middle of this part, usually not visited by the kayakers from higher up.

The valley is well-known for its wildlife, and you may well see golden eagle and short-eared owl in the daylight, as well as otter.

Access

A minor road, the B8074, follows the river most of the way down on its left bank, veering away only when the rapids are coming up. Access below the Falls of Orchy (NN 242 320; 56.4473, -4.8557). Egress downstream of the A85 road bridge (NN 138 282; 56.4092, -5.0218).

Campsites & accommodation

Tyndrum to the east, Bridge of Awe to the west.

Description

Km

0   Eas Urchaidh Falls. Good parking here. If in doubt, inspect the next kilometre of river, as there is a weir just downstream (0.5m drop), with a noticeable towback and some rock ledges. Inspect from left bank.

2   Footbridge, car parking. River flattens out, gravel banks and islands.

6   Grey shed and white house on left bank signals start of rapids. As the river flows around an island, both the left and right passages are blocked by boulders. Egress to road on left bank at this point (NN 202 285; 56.4144, -4.9182). There follows three drops over some 600m. Portage is possible through trees on left bank, but lining down nearly impossible due to trees and rocks. At medium to high water, the rapids are shootable, the only real difficulty being the high first drop. A rocky approach down left side of an island leads to an appreciable drop on right side of river, rocky shallows on left. Then a good

Connel sound and Connel Bridge, Loch Etive   📷 *Tony Hammock*

chute down the left side of next island follows, right side very dry, leading into a final drop on right side of river, which winds back to left of river, and a further 200m of shallow water.

7   At end of rapids, the River Lochy joins from left, good stopping place on right bank.

8.5 After a long quiet stretch, river disappears down a stony chute on right, banks of stones ahead. The chute runs straight into a tree, and traps debris, a common capsize site. Take care.

9.5 Dalmally village bridge. Access on right bank upstream of bridge. Shallows under the bridge. The river now becomes braided, with islands and banks of stones. No difficulties. River heads north-west, good views of Ben Cruachan.

11.5 On right bank, as river takes a left-hand bend around an island, notice the sand martin holes in sandy right bank.

12.5 A85(T) road bridge. Paddle down to the railway bridge 200m below, and land immediately under it on the left side, to egress on to a muddy track on the upstream side, another 200m or so from the

parking place. (This is a sharp turn off the A85, heading west, just before the road bridge, and is a private access to Kilchurn Castle on Loch Awe.)

065 Loch Awe

Length   Round trip of up to 72km
OS   50/55

Introduction
The loch is a massive 36km long, and offers a week of paddling with little trouble, especially if Loch Avich and the coast are explored as well. It is very 'Canadian' in appearance, with vast stretches of conifers.

Access
There is one problem, namely a frustrating lack of places to access the water, possibly intentional, to prevent those without licences from fishing. Access on at top end, below A85 road bridge, off track to Kilchurn Castle (NN 139 279; 56.4066, -5.0200); from the B846, on the west side, at North Port (NN 048 214; 56.3446, -5.1627); from Dalavich village, on the west side, behind the houses (NM 970 126; 56.2624, -5.2822), quite good vehicle parking; and from

Early morning on Loch Awe   📷 *Stuart Wagstaff*

Ford pier at the bottom end (NM 874 045; 56.1855, -5.4308), gate usually locked, but canoes can be carried over, and vehicle parked on a long passing place on the road above.

Campsites & accommodation
Bridge of Awe, otherwise wild sites in the forest areas. Once on the water, campsites can be found relatively easily, clearings in the forest being the item to look out for. (You will find the existing small camp and caravan sites are private ones for anglers). The long road down the east side has very few opportunities to access the water, and passing places must not be used for car parking or camping.

Description
There are many castles, historic sites, island burial grounds, and crannogs on the loch - go get a map and explore! This is one of the relatively few areas of Scotland where, as a paddler, you will be undisturbed and can paddle for hours or days.

Short easy trip
From the parking at Kilchurn Castle (NN 139 279; 56.4066, -5.0200), staying in the narrow north-east section of the loch. Paddle for 4km out and back to a crannog further south (NN 122 264; 56.3924, -5.0465).

066 Loch Avich

Length	Round trip of up to 10km
OS	55

Introduction
Loch Avich is worth a visit, a small piece of water on the west side, and higher up than Loch Awe.

Access
The loch has access from the minor road that runs from Loch Awe to Kilmelford, along its north side. There is a car park (NM 913 138; 56.2707, -5.3753) near a ruined castle on an island.

Campsites & accommodation
None local. The nearest are Asknish Bay to the west, on the coast, or Bridge of Awe.

Description
Loch Avich is 5km long, with access from the road on the north side. There is a car park near

a ruined castle on an island only a few metres off the mainland, which provides a useful base. The burn coming in at the top can be paddled up a couple of hundred metres. At the lower end is the exit of the River Avich (see *Scottish White Water*).

067 Loch Melfort and Nearby Islands

Length	Up to 40km
OS	55
Tides	Large areas dry out at LW

Distances
Many different trips can be run in this area, from short trips up to 30–40km circular expeditions.

Tides and weather
The western side of both Luing and Seil are very exposed to the weather, and tides run very fast through the Sound of Luing (Fladda).

Introduction
The islands of Seil, Luing, Torsa and Shuna are included because this is one of the most sheltered parts of the coastal islands, with plenty of paddling opportunities, if the prevailing weather conditions are taken into account.

Access
A base may be had on Seil, either near 'Atlantic Bridge' (Clachan Bridge NM 785 197; 56.3178, -5.5872), the very narrow channel between the island and mainland, or down at Balvicar Bay (NM 768 168; 56.2910, -5.6122). Other possibilities are to launch on Loch Melfort, the head of which is quite dry at low tide, or

at Craobh Haven, the marina (NM 795 075; 56.2088, -5.5608).

Campsites & accommodation
Asknish Bay on the coast, just south of Loch Melfort.

Description
Seil is fairly quiet and laid-back, with access south to Cuan Sound, through which the tide rushes, as with all narrow channels in this part of the world. Torsa is just across Cuan Sound, with the delightful Ardinamar Bay to the south.

Seil Sound runs inland of Seil for 8km down to Ardinamar, and it is 8km to the head of Loch Melfort, with a hotel and yacht anchorage and chandlers. The main hive of activity in the area is the newish marina of Craobh Haven, south of Loch Melfort, which was built within three natural islands. The marina has the usual facilities, including a pub with food open all day, a useful service in the area. It is perfectly possible from here to circumnavigate Shuna, in settled sea conditions, and explore the east side of Luing.

The western side of both Luing and Seil are very exposed to the weather, and tides run very fast through the Sound of Luing (Fladda).

Short easy trip
Balvicar to Atlantic Bridge and return – 6km. Leave Balvicar an hour before HW, returning from Atlantic Bridge on the first of the ebb. Otherwise, the paddler might well get stuck on seaweed and rocks.

Lochgilphead

River Add   📷 *Graham Warren*

Lochgilphead

This town is tiny, but it is the administrative and market centre for a large area, including the whole of the peninsula of Kintyre. In this part of Scotland, all distances are large! This area boasts Kilmartin Glen to the north, one of the most important geological and archaeological sites in Scotland, the Crinan Canal to the west, and the lovely Loch Sween and Tayvallich to the south. Even further south is the island of Gigha, off the west coast of Kintyre. This makes the whole area a tourist mecca, although it is still not as well-known or visited as areas to the north.

068 Loch Craignish

Length	12km
OS	55
Tides	Tidal streams negligible

Tides

Tidal streams are weak within the loch, but as soon as the paddler ventures outside the

mouth of the loch, much more tidal effect will be felt. The dreaded Corryvreckan tidal race is only 6 km to the north-west, from the mouth of the loch.

Introduction

This is a reasonably safe and interesting sea loch, ideally placed near both Loch Awe to the east, and the Crinan area to the south. The loch is well sheltered from the west, has islands off its mouth on the open sea, and also islands within it. The only conditions to avoid are when a south-westerly swell runs directly into the loch.

Access

Ardfern, a major yachting centre, is the main inhabited area. As with many canoeing areas, parking of vehicles can be a problem. The B8002 runs down the northern shore, but the only parking places are in Ardfern itself, near the hotel (NM 804 041; 56.1788, -5.5434), down at the bottom end around Bagh Dun Mhullig (NM 778 019; 56.1578, -5.5835), a sandy bay, or over the headland in Loch Beag around Craignish Castle (NM 765 006; 56.1456, -5.6034).

Campsites & accommodation
Asknish Bay to the north.

Description
The loch is 6km long, and a round trip between the islands is well worthwhile. The east side is much quieter than the west, which is busy with yachts in the summer. Eilean Righ, the largest island, has plenty of pleasant stopping places. Crossing the loch is perhaps safest between Bagh Dun Mhuilig and the southern end of Eilean Righ.

Short easy trip
From Ardfern, (NM 804 041; 56.1788, -5.5434) paddle north to the inland end of the loch, and around Eilean Mhic Chrion, the long narrow island off Ardfern, a total of 8km.

069 River Add and Loch Crinan

Length	Up to 13.5km
OS	55
Grade	1
Tides	See below

Distances
Round trip of either 6 or 8km on Loch Crinan; River Add is 5.5km.

Tides
There are fast tidal streams here and paddlers could be left on dry sand, so it is essential to look at tide tables before attempting the trip. The trip needs to be timed so that you enter the loch from the river at near high tide, and use the ebb to go seawards.

Introduction
The small Loch Crinan is the entrance to the Crinan Canal. Crinan Harbour is between an island and the mainland, and the River Add flows into it. One of the main reasons for visiting this area would be Kilmartin Glen, of which the River Add and the surrounding area are important parts, as this was a major gateway into Scotland from Ireland in both pre-Christian and medieval times.

Access
From the B841 alongside the Crinan Canal, to Islandadd Bridge (NR 804 925; 56.0747, -5.5338), or the Crinan Canal basin (NR 789 944; 56.0911, -5.5595).

Campsites & accommodation
Camping near the Bellanoch Hotel, just after Islandadd Bridge.

Description
The Add is quite possible from the road to Dunadd, the obvious hill fort which rises over the very flat plain of Moine Mhor, and it flows a very winding 5.5km into the estuary at Islandadd Bridge. 1.5km of sandy / muddy estuary follows until Crinan Ferry, a very obvious ferry point, now disused but of historic interest.

The area of Moine Mhor is the southern part of Kilmartin Glen, with enough cairns, stone circles and cup and ring rocks to keep anybody happy. It is really worthwhile to start at the museum and take a guided tour of the area.

070 Crinan Canal

Length	14.5km
OS	55

Portages

Portages around four sets of locks (15 locks in all).

Introduction

This canal is 'Scotland's most beautiful short-cut', the 14.5km-long waterway cutting off the 160km trip around the Mull of Kintyre. There are 15 locks, in four groups, leading to four portages, and seven bridges.

Access

There are many options off the B841 which runs alongside the canal to Crinan, the westerly entrance, especially near the locks. Egress at Ardrishaig (NR 852 852; 56.0115, -5.4508) on the A83 road down the east coast of Kintyre.

Campsites & accommodation

At Tayvallich and Lochgilphead, plus at Bellanoch on the canal.

Description

The canal runs west to east from Crinan village, past Lochgilphead, to the sea at Ardrishaig. The useful campsite in the centre of Lochgilphead can be reached by a short portage.

Go to the very informative website: *www.scottishcanals.com* for full details.

Short easy trip

Crinan village to east, and back – various distances up to 6km.

071 Tayvallich and Loch Sween

Length	Round trip up to 34km
OS	62/55
Tides	See below

Tides

The inlets at the head of the loch are only possible at high tide, and any trip out from Tayvallich should commence at say an hour and a half before high tide, giving a trip of three hours or so, using the flood going and the ebb returning. Tayvallich at low tide is not pleasant, with much mud. If heading out down the loch from Tayvallich, start at high tide and use the ebb. Castle Sween is an obvious destination 10km down, and would be reached before the tide is half way out (HW plus 3 hours).

Introduction

This area has much for paddlers – a very sheltered top end of Loch Sween with inlets to explore, the village of Tayvallich, a yachting centre and harbour, and the Sound of Jura under a kilometre to the west at Carsaig. In recent years Eurasian beavers have been Introduced under licence by the Scottish Wildlife Trust, and are in a freshwater loch to the north of the top of Loch Sween. Look for signs.

Access

The B8025 runs from the Crinan Canal to Tayvallich (NR 740 872; 56.0242, -5.6323), and a side road leaves this to follow the east side of Loch Sween down to Castle Sween (NR 715 790; 55.9495, -5.6654).

Campsites & accommodation

At Tayvallich and Castle Sween.

Description

The loch is 17km from its head out to the McCormaig Islands, which can be reached in calm weather.

The head has three inlets to paddle. Caol Scotnish gives the experience of both sea and woodland habitat, a heronry in the forest, and woodland birds on rocks in the tidal area. It is not surprising that this wet and wooded habitat was chosen as a beaver habitat.

Around the corner on the main loch are the Fairy Islands on the west side, an area of lagoons, sandbars and wooded islands, all peaceful and worth exploring.

About two-thirds of the way down Loch Sween is Castle Sween, a caravan and campsite, with shop. Speedboats may be encountered around here.

On the opposite, west side are two large inlets, both quite hidden. Caol Scotnish is behind Taynich Island and the Ulva Islands. A paddlecraft can of course push its nose through narrow passages and shallow water. Further south is the Island of Danna, not obviously an island but circumnavigable in calm conditions.

Eilean Mor, the largest of the four McCormaigs, is well worth a visit. At one point in history, this was a 'motorway' stop for the sea traffic between Ireland and Scotland, and so it is not surprising that a saint made his home here – the cave, chapel and cross can all be seen.

Short easy trip

Tayvallich bay round trip – 2km.

072 West Loch Tarbert

Length	14km or round trip of up to 28km
OS	62
Tides	See below

Tides

Trips are only possible from the head of the loch at Tarbert at high tide, as there are large drying areas. Kennacraig (small ferry port 4km), or Ronachan Point, on A83 (a further 7km), could be reached on an ebb tide for a one-way trip.

Introduction

This is the most southerly paddling recommended in this area, and this loch has two things going for it: it has a genuinely short and possible portage from the town of Tarbert over the neck of land to the west, and a very convenient campsite just where you might want to embark.

Access

From the A83, which follows the loch down its east side. Access on at the top (NR 843 664; 55.8424, -5.4501) near the campsite. Egress on to a small road off the B8024 on the west side at a bay near the mouth with the sea (NR 755 595; 55.7766, -5.5851).

Campsites & accommodation

Near the head of the loch (Tarbert).

Description

There have been open canoe trips down Loch Fyne, overland west at Tarbert, and up to Loch Killisport or Loch Sween, but, as always, very settled weather is required. The portage is 1.5km, and the loch is 14km long. The paddle is fairly sheltered out as far as Ardpatrick Point, and one good tour is to round the point to Loch Stornoway (3km).

Crinan Canal, eastern entrance Stuart Wagstaff

Cowal

Ben Lomond reflected in Loch Lomond   📷 *Carol Pudsey*

Cowal

Cowal is the name for the land west and north of Glasgow, the southerly part of Argyll with very long road communication, and long and mainly wooded peninsulas. Although a favourite for a long time with the population of Glasgow, the area is relatively unknown to many visitors to Scotland – the paddling possibilities are good, both around the islands and up the long lochs.

Dunoon is the main town on Cowal but, unless the ferry from Glasgow is taken, the road journey is enormous, being about 70 miles from Dumbarton on the Firth of Clyde.

073 Loch Fyne

Length	The loch is 65km long
OS	62/55/56
Tides	Tidal streams negligible

Introduction

This is a very long loch which makes up the east side of the peninsula of Kintyre. Interest is probably more in short day trips out from various access points on the loch.

Access

From Ardrishaig or Lochgilphead on the west side, Inveraray further north, or other possible landing points off the A83 road. The east side is much less inhabited, with few roads. Otter Ferry is the most southerly practicable access point on the east, a minor road running up its shore to join the Rothesay road near Strachur.

Campsites & accommodation

At Lochgilphead, and two sites just south of Inveraray.

Description

Interest for paddlers probably starts at Tarbert, with Ardrishaig (Crinan Canal) 17km to the north. Around the headland protecting Lochgilphead, Loch Fyne heads north-east, Otter Ferry on the east shore (Cowal), being another 8km. The loch narrows to some 1.5–2km wide, and the A83 mainly follows the west shore. It is a long 30km up to Inveraray, the most important town on this stretch of coast, and a further 10km to the head of the loch. From near here, the main road crosses Cowal by the 'Rest and be Thankful' pass to Arrochar, and Tarbet on Loch Lomond.

Other important points

From Strachur, on the east side, it is a 7km portage (possibly using also the River Cur) over to the narrow, 10km long Loch Eck, which has been used in the past to reach Holy Loch, down the River Eachaig. This is a beautiful area with good campsites, and it is quiet and isolated.

074 Isle of Bute and Nearby Lochs

Length	Up to 25km
OS	63
Tides	See below

Distances

Loch Ruel is 5km long, Loch Striven 13km long. A round trip down one loch, along the Kyles of Bute, and up the other loch is 25km.

Tides

The tides are noticeable at obvious narrows, e.g. around the Kyles of Bute, which is the name for the narrows around the north-west and north-east of the island. Lochs Ruel and Striven to the north, dry out for long distances at low tide, and landings on Bute at low tide can be seaweedy.

Introduction

This is the outermost part of the Firth of Clyde which is suitable for paddlecraft other

Loch Ruel 　　　　　　　　　　　　　　📷 *Eddie Palmer*

than specialist sea kayaks. Bute may be circumnavigated, but the west coast can be rocky, with no roads. The east side is more sheltered, with more habitation, but also more disturbances. The island is more than 50km in circumference. The islands of Great Cumbrae and Little Cumbrae are off to the east, the latter being rocky and exposed. This area is described in one section, because a trip or holiday may be taken in the general area.

Access

From Rothesay on Bute, reached by ferry from Wemyss Bay, or by A866 road from Strachur, which follows the Kyle down to its end at Strone Point (NS 075 714; 55.8971, -5.0828).

Campsites & accommodation

No known formal sites in the immediate area.

Description

Loch Ruel is to the north of Bute, only 0.5km away, being 5km long, half of which dries out at low tide. The Kyle is interesting, with islands and shallows. Scenery good in the whole area, very wooded.

Loch Striven is 13km long, a narrow loch which is quite isolated, there being no road up the west side.

075 Lochs Long, Goil, Holy Loch and Gare Loch

Length	Up to 42km
OS	56/63
Tides	Tidal streams weak

Tides

Tidal streams are weak and of little concern but landing at low water can make for tiresome long carries.

Introduction

These lochs represent the more interesting and useful paddling in the area of the upper Firth of Clyde. Take note! All can be affected by naval operations, usually submarine exercises. The normally restricted area is on the east side of Loch Long covering the Coulport area. All that paddlers have to do is avoid this area by crossing over to the west bank well in time. If following the east bank, head across at Peaton Layo (NS 214 860; 56.0335, -4.8700) to Ardentinny and keep to the west bank until Loch Goil.

Access

The head of Loch Long is reached on the A83, or A814 from Tarbet on Loch Lomond. The B828 and B839 end up at Lochgoilhead, a good base for a trip in these parts.

Campsites & accommodation

Lochgoilhead, and Gairletter Point, south of Ardentinny on Loch Long. Ardgarten, at the top of Loch Long.

Description

Holy Loch is the most westerly of this foursome, just around the corner from Dunoon, 3.5km long, and heavily populated. It does lead, however, by a portage to Loch Eck inland.

Loch Long is as it sounds, very long, 26km from its entrance opposite Gourock on the Clyde up to Arrochar, from whence a portage may be made over to Loch Lomond. The round trip, in settled weather, from Lomond down the River Leven to the Clyde, along to Loch Long, and over the Arrochar neck back to Loch Lomond, is a long-established touring route. It is a 3-day trip.

The first part of Loch Long has roads both sides, but these finish at Ardentinny on the west side, and Coulport on the east, after the first 6km. After another 5km Loch Goil opens out up to the north-west, a gem of an area for touring. This is a very attractive and wooded 8km loch, well worth exploring. The head of the loch at Lochgoilhead is a good base, with a large campsite. Loch Long then stretches for a further 14km to the head, where the main A83 winds around it.

Gare Loch is very busy, and almost industrialised for its 10km length, with the town of Helensburgh, the marina at Rhu, and then the major naval base at Faslane. It is probably best avoided with so many other pleasant cruising grounds nearby.

077 Loch Lomond

Length	Up to 72km
OS	56

Introduction

This famous and beautiful loch is a great favourite with canoeists and kayakers, and offers one of the best and most interesting stretches of fresh water in Britain. The loch is large, with both large and small islands and so the paddling possibilities are endless. A week's

Loch Lomond *Sue Tadman*

holiday can easily be spent on it, and the West Highland Way also follows the east bank.

Since 2003 Loch Lomond has been part of the Loch Lomond and Trossachs National Park, although the main change noticed by local paddlers has been an increase in speedboats and jet skis which are a menace, although mainly on weekends in high summer.

Much of the shoreline of Loch Lomond now has bye-laws, banning 'wild' or informal camping during the summer, with a licensing system for wild camping on designated sites. This prohibition is strictly enforced. There is however, along with the Cashel and Milarrochy camp sites on the east side, a new site at Sallochy, about halfway down the loch. This policy is very controversial, and still being challenged. The paddler should visit the LL&T Park website to discover any annual changes to the rules.

Access

The loch is also quite varied in character, the northerly 'narrow end' being much quieter as well than the 'bulge' at the southern end, and the fleshpots of Balloch. A main road (A82)

follows the west bank, while on the east side a road only goes as far as Rowardennan, leading to Ben Lomond, and the famous Youth Hostel there. This means that the east side has quite a few attractions.

Campsites & accommodation

Camping can be difficult, but main sites are mentioned. The islands are, however, not yet covered by the bye-laws, and canoeists enjoy good camping on them.

Description

The loch is 36km long, 6km wide in some places, and over 550m deep. With winds being mainly from the south-west, the fetch can be large, and waves high at times. The weather is also very unpredictable, the loch being surrounded by mountains, and very fast-changing weather. A day trip out to islands should be made with this knowledge in mind. The 30 islands have castles, monuments, and many points of interest. This is a real tourist treat, and so the paddler should take time and explore. Some distances are set out below with some hints for visits.

Km

0   Ardlui - the top of the loch, with access now difficult onto the loch. Launch to the River Falloch about 2km up from the village, much easier. Going south. The A82 road follows the west bank.

3   I Vow Island. Castle.

5.5   Rob Roy's Cave on left bank.

6.5   Inveruglas Isle to right, Castle.

7.5   Inversnaid on left (east) bank. Gateway to the Trossach lochs. Pier and hotel.

12.5   Tarbet on right bank. Three kilometre portage west to Loch Long. Hotels, shops, pier.

18.5   Rowardennan Lodge (Youth Hostel) on left bank.

19.5   Rowardennan Hotel and car park, picnic site on left bank. Inverbeg on right bank. Caravan site and pier.

25.5   Ross Point on left. Loch narrows for a final time. Ross Islands to left. Sallochy camp site on east bank

28   On right bank (west) Luss village, shops, pier, sandy beach. To south, Inchlonaig Island. To south-east (east bank) – Cashel campsite (Forest Enterprise). Beach, landing, room for boats and canoes.

30   On west side, south from Luss, Aldochlay village. South from Inchlonaig, six islands in the centre of the loch; west to east: Inchtavannach, the 'Lagoon', interesting narrow passage between it and Inchconnachan (the wallaby island – wallabies were released here some years ago); Inchmoan, with good sandy beaches, and Inchgalbraith, a crannog to the south of it; a very narrow and shallow passage between it and Inchcruin, and then Bucinch off to the north; to the east again, Inchfad, with Ellendarroch off its west end, another crannog.

30.5   On east side, Strathcashel Point, then Milarrochy Bay (campsite), with boathouse for Loch Lomond Sailing Club, which houses many sailing canoes.

31   On west side Bandry Bay, look out for the statue in the water.

31.5   South from Inchfad:
Five islands in a line from NE to SW, Inchcailloch, a nature reserve, with a campsite, viewpoint on its hill, chapel at east end; land at sandy bay near west end. This island well worth visiting.

33   On east side Balmaha village, with marina, shops, cafés, hotels.

There follows Clairinsh, behind and to the south of Inchcailloch, Torrinch to the southwest and Creinch, again to south-west.

It is unlikely that the paddler will really want to go south of these islands, as near Balloch, the speedboat traffic increases greatly.

Inchmurrin is to the south, with a pier, castle, and hotel, the largest island.

To the west are a number of private properties with little landing or egress. There is a jetty due west of the Inchmurrin jetty, and another 2km further south at Arden House.

Cameron House Hotel is 1.5km nearer to Balloch, followed by the new Loch Lomond Shores shopping centre.

Balloch, as hinted at above, can be very busy with many boat movements. It has shopping, and a country park on the east bank.

The River Leven leaves the loch through a very congested boat area, and then a weir prevents the motorised boats going any further south. The river winds for 9km through an urban area to the Clyde (risk of children throwing stones), with the latter third tidal. It is only recommended for transit to the Clyde.

Short easy trip
Balmaha to Luss and return – 12km.

077 Loch Lomond, River Leven, Firth of Clyde and Loch Long

Length	81km
OS	56/63
Grade	1
Tides	Tidal streams weak

Portages
A portage on the River Leven, down the barrier/weir below Balloch; a portage of 2.5km from Arrochar to Tarbet, between Loch Long and Loch Lomond.

Tides and weather
Tidal streams in the Firth of Clyde and Loch Long are weak and of little concern. They are exposed to bad weather and a stable weather forecast is important.

Introduction
An absolutely classic trip, carried out many times by the Open Canoe Sailing Group. It involves every type of paddling and sailing. See Route 075 concerning MoD restricted areas.

Access
Usually started on Loch Lomond, either at Tarbet or Balloch.

Campsites & accommodation
Various places described in the text will enable you to have a quiet night and avoid habitation.

Description
This route has been mainly covered in the other trips in the Cowal section. There are few difficulties apart from the exposure of the Firth of Clyde, and the fact that the River Leven is not amongst the most pleasant.
The distances are:
    Tarbet to Balloch - 22km.
    Balloch to Dumbarton - 12km.
    Dumbarton to Ardmore, (possible campsite) after Cardross -10km.
    Ardmore, across mouth of Gare Loch to Rosneath Point (stopping place or campsite) - 5km - on to Loch Long - 5km.
    Loch Long to Arrochar - 25km (many camping possibilities on Loch Long).
    Arrochar, portage across to Tarbet - 2.5km.

Other important points
Time taken will be three (hard) days minimum, four or five days would be more enjoyable, and the weather might make this necessary.

078 Endrick Water

Length	8km
OS	56/57
Grade	1

Water levels
On SEPA gauge, into the 'Medium' level

Introduction
The Endrick is small, and probably only of local interest, but many visitors to Loch Lomond have attempted it. It rises miles to the east in the Stirlingshire hills above Fintry.

Endrick Water in the autumn 📷 *Robert Craig*

Access

Normal access is at Drymen Bridge (NS 473 873; 56.0541, -4.4548), reached by the road through Drymen.

There is a possible higher access point, rarely used due to low water levels, at Gartness, but there is a water fall near the start. Take the A809 towards Glasgow, and then the B834 off to the east, A81 north and then a sideroad to Gartness (NS 501 868; 56.0505, -4.4096) The lower part of the river can be seen from the road most of the way.

Campsites & accommodation

Balmaha on Loch Lomond.

Description

This is a pleasant and winding little river amongst very pastoral countryside remind-ing one of a southern English river. A trip is eminently possible from the road bridge near Drymen, the 7km down to Loch Lomond, where a further 1km paddle would bring you northwards to the harbour at Balmaha. The more usual trip by paddlers is to launch from Balmaha, and proceed upriver until it becomes too shallow

079 - River Clyde
Strathclyde to Glasgow

Length	29 or 33km
OS	64
Grade	1 (2)

Introduction

This is an interesting trip, commencing in surprisingly rural surroundings near Glasgow, flowing through quite a barren area of old industrial workings around Cambuslang, becoming tidal and then entering an obviously revitalised area around the former 2014 Commonwealth Games village in the east end of the city.

Access

Start at Strathclyde Country Park (NS 730 565; 55.7851, -4.0274 – access on to the river behind the main Park buildings, with café and changing facilities). The finish can either be at the pleasant Glasgow Green (NS 600 639; 55.8479, -4.2386), a playground for the city, or further downstream at Kelvin Harbour slipway (NS 556 659; 55.8646, -4.3100).

Campsites

Strathclyde Country Park

Description

The weir at Carmyle is a grade 2 and the tidal limit is passed above Glasgow centre, the water being held back by a weir further downstream. Below Glasgow Green, the paddler is on more flowing tidal water, and a trip on the first of the ebb tide is recommended.

Km

0   Strathclyde Country Park

5   High weir by the David Livingstone

River Clyde at Bothwell *Jim Wallis*

Memorial Centre at Blantyre, to be portaged on the right bank. The river continues past the dramatic Bothwell Castle after which the greenery has more old industrial remains hidden in it, remnants of once-thriving iron and steel workings.

15 Carmyle weir – can be shot anywhere, but do not enter overflow channel river right. Portage on right bank. The A763 road bridge is overhead.

18 M74 bridge at about.

20 'The Loop', river turns to the left around a sharp loop, left bank now a country park. New housing to the right

24 The Clyde becomes tidal, not usually obvious except for muddy banks at low tides. Rowing clubs on the river at certain times of day and week.

29 – Glasgow Green, egress possible at steps and pontoons of the rowing clubs (NS 00 639; 55.8479, -4.2386).

It is now possible to portage the weir ahead, either by lifting over fences on the side of the river, or at low flows to use the boarding over the extreme right side of the weir, there for rowing boats etc.

You are now in the centre of Glasgow! No ships, but plenty else to see.

33 Only possible place to land, and finish is the Kelvin Harbour slipway, river right, recognised by it being just downstream of the new Transport Museum, and the tied-up schooner, Glen Lee. Best to paddle down the last 4km between an hour before, and an hour after, High Water. There is plenty of parking at the Transport Museum.

080 River Clyde
Glasgow to Dumbarton

Length	21km
OS	64 and 63
Tides	Extensive mud banks at LW

Introduction

A pleasant trip down an interesting river, with many historical and industrial features. As shipping has declined, the river has become

River Clyde by Havoc Road Park, Dumbarton 📷 *Jim Wallis*

safer for small craft. After the Erskine Bridge, the most down river road bridge, the estuary becomes more exposed, and so the prevailing weather has to be taken into account

Description

This section is tidal and the 21km will need to be paddled to arrive at Sandpoint Marina, Dumbarton on a rising tide. Assuming the distance takes about 4 hours, one could leave on an ebb tide at half tide, so that on arrival the tide will be rising, so avoiding the mud in the estuary at low tide.

0 – Leave Kelvin harbour(NS 556 659; 55.8646, -4.3100). You are now in a port, and so access legislation does not apply. Peel Holdings, the port authority, Issue guidance in 'Clyde Leisure Navigation Guide' ... 'Be safe, Be seen'.

7 – Yoker ferry slip on right bank (NS 511 685; 55.8866, -4.3834) – only possible stopping point on this stretch, due to vertical river walls.

13.5 – As the Erskine Bridge is nearly overhead, there is landing on left bank at the slipway and car park, a very useful facility (NS 402 721; 55.9154, -4.5598).

The Clyde now starts to widen out, but beware, the dredged channel for any shippjng is very narrow, and you could encounter barges and tugs. They will not be able to manouvre to avoid you! Keep well in to the right side of the river all the way down - the mud flats on the south side can trap an unwary paddler.

Bowling Harbour, and the entrance to the Forth and Clyde Canal is river right, 2km after the bridge. Dunglas Castle then follows on the right bank, and Dumbarton Rock, and its castle, are very obvious ahead.

20 – At Dumbarton, turn in to the River Leven.

21 – Sandpoint Marina is on the opposite (west) bank of the river from the castle. (NS 396 748; 55.9394, -4.5710)

Other important points

This trip can be extended along the north bank of the Clyde. Ardmore Point Is a further 11k on, with camping possibilities and then Helensburgh is another 6km.

The Deveron near Huntley 📷 Mike Forres

East

Contents

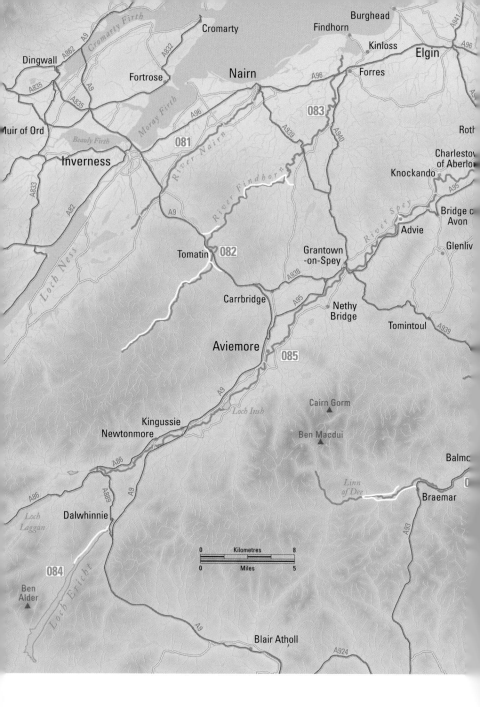

Moray and Grampian

Mains of Sluie, Lower Findhorn   ⬜ *Greg Davies*

Moray and Grampian

This eastern part of Scotland is relatively un-known and less touristy, as it is mainly a quiet agricultural area. The advantage for the pad-dler is that there are often empty roads, and miles of lovely scenery. Another major plus for the paddler is that the gradual descent east from the main watershed mean that there are several long rivers in this area, giving many miles of paddling.

081 River Nairn

Length	27km
OS	27
Grade	1–2

Introduction

The Nairn is a little-known and underused river, flowing down a delightful valley. It rises on the western side of the Monadhliath, above the 'Scottish Lake District' around the eastern side of Loch Ness, and flows north-east to the sea at Nairn town. It's a useful day trip either when other rivers are too high, or the sea is too rough.

Water Level

Look at any bridge, but especially the B9090 – the river can be paddled if there is enough water over the shingle rapids.

Access

The Nairn passes under the main A9 road, and access and parking is at the old road bridge east of the current road (NH 721 388; 57.4215, -4.1322). There is also access/egress at next road bridge (NH 742 430; 57.4598, -4.0993), Clava Lodge Hotel bridge (NH 759 448; 57.4764, -4.0719), Cantray Bridge (NH 800 480; 57.5062, -4.0051), the B9090 road bridge near Cawdor, and Howford bridge (NH 876 538; 57.5603, -3.8809).

Final egress is in Nairn, where the last bridge carries the A96 (NH 886 566; 57.5857, -3.8655), or in the harbour (dry at low tide).

Campsites & accommodation

Newlands, near Culloden, at Nairn beach, east of the town or at Househill, just south of Nairn.

Description
The Nairn proceeds north-east 27km to the sea at Nairn town, a long trip for one day, although it can of course be shortened. It is an easy grade 1–2, requiring recent rain to make it worthwhile. Little wooded gorges are interspersed with wider, braided stretches with gravel islands. Access / egress only at five road bridges down the valley. The fourth one (the B9090) is possibly a better start point for an open canoe, due to numerous trees across the river in the upper stretches.

Other important points
The river passes very close to the Culloden Moor battleground, well worth visiting for its atmosphere.

082 Upper Findhorn

Length	27km
OS	27/35
Grade	1–2 (2–3)

Grade
Grade 1–2 (but some of the river is very isolated, increasing the seriousness of the grade). Some rapids can be grade 2–3 in high water.

Introduction
Yes, this is 'The' Findhorn, which has an upper valley of some length, and a canoeing possibility of a long day trip above the white water sections in the difficult upper and lower gorges. This upper valley has been ignored in favour of the superb stretches of white water lower down, but egress is possible before Dulsie Rapid, the usual start of the 'Upper

Findhorn' white water. Perhaps one reason is that no road follows some 12km of the river.

Water Level
The river is shallow and shingly. A look over the bridge at Findhorn Bridge should save unnecessary driving, the level will be obvious.

Access
At Tomatin, on the A9 (heading north), turn off for Drumbain and Morile on a side road just after the Slochd summit. At Findhorn Bridge (NH 803 277; 57.3241, -3.9902) cross the river, look at the level, which should be obvious, and head up the valley. The river is wide, flat and shallow. The valley is flat-bottomed, and very remote – there often being no signs of life in this stalking and shooting area.

If there is water at all, the river will be doable from Garbole (NH 758 245; 57.2942, -4.0633), where a tributary enters. There is a large lay-by here for parking.

Egress for this stretch is near Banchor (NH 908 403; 57.4399, -3.8213), upstream of Dulsie Bridge (the usual start for white-water trips).

Campsites & accommodation
None nearby. Carrbridge or Aviemore would be the best bets.

Description
Km
0   Start where the tributary enters at Garbole.
2.5   Large islands.
7.5   Findhorn Bridge - good parking on the bridge where strange concrete abutments have been built. There is now a choice of going on to the near take-out, some 7.5km downstream at Ruthven, easily

reached by road, or on to Carnoch, 25km, and a vehicle shuttle of at least 26 miles!

8.5 Railway bridge, followed by A9 bridge, both very high above valley. River bends considerably, always near the A9.

14 Tributary enters left. Just after this, a road comes alongside on the left, and there is also a parking space on the left bank. (The rest of the road only has passing places – this road comes down from the A9 at Dalmagarry).

15 Ruthven hamlet on left. Road finishes, and hills close in. River remains of same character, rapids maybe grade 2–3 in high water.

17.5 'Sheep trolley' crosses the river on rope-way. Shennachie ruin on left.

18 Long bend to right. River narrows and speeds up.

22.5 Approaching sharp bend to left, Daless Farm is high on hill to the left, first road, and egress in emergency.

24 Bridge. Drynachan Lodge on left bank. Road now follows left bank.

25 Carnoch to left.

27 Road is right alongside river – this is easiest place to egress from this trip, and is 2km upriver from Banchor.

The Findhorn now starts to speed up and become more difficult. Dulsie Rapid is 2.5km further down ... go and have a look at it from Dulsie Bridge.

Other important points

Just to make this even more interesting, the more conventional (white water) upper and middle reaches have been done by open canoe, with just a couple of portages, plus the bottom end below the Lower Gorge from Mains of Sluie down to the sea at Findhorn. If inter-

ested, see the *Scottish White Water* guide, but this is an advanced trip!

083 Lower Findhorn

Below Sluie Gorge

Length	15.5km
OS	27
Grade	1–2
Tides	Strong tidal streams in estuary

Introduction

A beautiful trip, amongst the same staggering scenery as the rest of the Lower Findhorn, ending at Findhorn village, across the estuary.

Water Level

Look upstream at A96 road bridge – the steepish rapid upstream should have enough water not to be a scrape.

Access

From the A940, Grantown to Forres road, where the car park for the Mains of Sluie walks are signposted (NJ 013 523; 57.5500, -3.6512), at the main A96 road bridge (NJ 011 581; 57.6020, -3.6569), and at Findhorn harbour (NJ 038 645; 57.6601, -3.6143).

Campsites & accommodation

Mundole, on the river, and at Findhorn (two sites).

Description

Km

0 Launch at Mains of Sluie, where the lower gorge ends. Vehicles can be taken down to the old farmhouse (now renovated as holiday accommodation, please show

regard for others here), drop off your boats and use the car park near the main road. This paddle is a glorious one in an easy, wooded, red sandstone gorge.

4   Where the river finally straightens out, after sharp bends and cliffs, you come to the Meads of St John on the left bank – beautiful ancient trees.

7   Mundole caravan park on right bank, possible egress.

8   Findhorn Bridge on A96 – parking and egress on the right upstream of bridge. There is now the option of entering the Findhorn estuary, which runs fast, and leaves large sandbanks at low tide. **Only attempt this in high water, and on the last of the flood tide.**

9   Railway bridge.

13   River enters estuary proper. Head across north to Findhorn village (obvious).

15.5 Findhorn harbour. Campsites at both the village and at the Findhorn Foundation, a mile inland.

084 Loch Ericht

Length	Round trip of up to 52km
OS	42
Icons	Inland Loch

Introduction
Loch Ericht is included here because, at least geographically, it makes sense to include it with the Spey, the loch being almost the most central loch in Scotland. It actually drains out both north to the Truim, a Spey tributary, and south into the River Ericht, a Tummel and Tay system tributary.

Access
From the north, from Dalwhinnie on the A9

Canoe sailing on Loch Ericht   Liam McKeown

to the dam at the north end (NN 632 843; 56.9297, -4.2504).

There is also an estate road to the south end (from Bridge of Ericht on Loch Rannoch), which is barred by a locked gate in a deer fence, and although access is allowed at some times, much frustration is caused by paddlers arriving and finding it locked. There is no logical system in place at time of writing.

Campsites & accommodation
Wild camping on the loch. The nearest sites are at Dalwhinnie or Newtonmore.

Description
The loch is a summer favourite for open canoeists wanting some peace and quiet, and offers 26km of an often windswept vista. It is used for mountain access to Ben Alder, which dominates the west side. The Rannoch Forest mountains are to the south-west, and the Drumochter hills to the east.

Campsites are easy to find, the infrequent little bays offering shelter.

Down near the southern end, on the west side is Alder Bay, with Ben Alder Cottage, a bothy, and Bonnie Prince Charlie's cave above it.

River Spey *Pete White*

085 River Spey

Length	114km
OS	35/36/28
Grade	1(2)

Grades

Grade 1, apart from grade 2 rapids at Grantown, Blacksboat, and Knockando to Carron Bridge.

Introduction

Yes, one of the 'Big Four' rivers that is a must for the touring canoeist in Scotland, and which normally provides a fast current, great scenery, and some interesting rapids.

The Spey is also a strange river in that much of the flow in the upper reaches is taken off by the Laggan dam scheme, taking water west from the watershed. The river is rarely paddled from up by Laggan village, it is usually

started from either Newtonmore or Kingussie. Many prefer to start from the Loch Insh Centre (which was founded by Clive Freshwater, who won the famous River Spey access court case in the 70s) but this would miss out the Insh marshes, which are worth seeing.

The Spey can easily be paddled in two and a half days in medium water from Newtonmore, but on high winter days, the river from the Avon junction down to the sea can be paddled (all 40km of it!) easily in a day by either kayak or canoe.

In recent years, middle summer levels have meant a deal of wading for parties of open canoeists, many feeling that the river is losing water, probably due to abstraction, but it is still a great experience, with the definite feeling that the river speeds up near the sea.

The river is described from Newtonmore, with campsites in the itinerary. Day trips on parts of the river are also well worthwhile.

Possible Itineraries

1) Newtonmore (campsite) to Aviemore (campsite) – 29km.
   Aviemore to Blackboats (campsite, booked in advance) – 35km.
   Blackboats to Spey Bay (campsite) – 40km.
2) Loch Insh (accom.) to Boat of Balliefurth – 31.5km.
   Balliefurth to Blackboats – 24.5km or Boat of Fiddich, Craigellachie campsite – 35.5km.
   To Spey Bay, either 40, or 29km.

Short easy trips

Loch Insch to Aviemore (grade 1) – 10km.
Blacksboat bridge to Aberlour (grade 2) – 11km.
Boat O'Brig to Spey Bay (grade 1) – 14km.

Water Level

Look at level at Newtonmore and Kingussie. There should be enough depth over the gravel rapids. Using the Where's the Water website calibration, the river should be above the minimum 'Medium' level.

Access

The Spey is a fine river for both paddlers and anglers, and can be crowded in places. Please keep to the following access and egress points, and take heed of advice:
Newtonmore (NN 709 997; 57.0702, -4.1318),
Kingussie Bridge (NN 709 997; 57.0702, -4.1318),
Loch Insch, left side, via track under railway bridge (NN 822 043; 56.2166, -3.9017),
Aviemore Old Bridge, pub downstream (NN 94 118; 56.2857, -3.7887),
Boat of Garten Bridge (NH 946 191; 57.2504, -3.7489),
Broomhill bridge (NN 996 224; 56.3832, -3.6279),
Boat of Balliefirth campsite (NJ 013 245; 57.3004, -3.6400),
Grantown on Spey (NJ 028 266; 57.3196, -3.6160),
Cromdale bridge (NJ 066 289; 57.3410, -3.5537),
Dellefure Burn (NJ 085 316; 57.3656, -3.5231),
Advie bridge (NJ 120 354; 57.4005, -3.4663),
Ballindalloch parking area (known also as Dalnapot NJ 169 368; 57.4140, -3.3852),
Blacksboat Bridge (NJ 184 389; 57.4331, -3.3610),
Knockando (NJ 190 416; 57.4574, -3.3519),
Carron Bridge (NJ 225 411; 57.4536, -3.2934),
Aberlour (NJ 262 429; 57.4703, -3.2322),
Boat O'Brig (NJ 318 517; 57.5502, -3.1413),
Fochabers Bridge (NJ 341 596; 57.6215, -3.1050),
Spey Bay (NJ 348 654; 57.6737, -3.0949).

Description

Km

0   Spey Bridge campsite, (NN 709 980; 57.0549, -4.1309) Newtonmore (just off the A9). The village is 0.5km north. If the river is obviously very dry, consider starting 8km further downstream. Rapid just below campsite. Railway bridge. The river is small, with gravel banks and islands. Access either left bank below bridge if using campsite, or right bank.

8   Kingussie Bridge (NN 760 997; 57.0716, -4.0476). By now, you're exhausted, and thinking this will take a week! However the river is deeper and faster from here. Access right bank, below Ruthven road bridge.

River Spey   📷 *Bridget Thomas*

9   A9 bridge. River enters Insh marshes, and scenery widens out. If low, view is obscured by high banks; if high, river is out over the marshes. There is a huge amount of bird life.

17   River enters Loch Insh. There is an access point on the left bank, which can be seen from either land or water, by an arch under a railway bridge. This is at the side of the Kingussie to Insch road. The watersports centre is obvious on right bank (NN 838 045; 56.2188, -3.8759). Landing, bar, restaurant, lodges for rent. You may well be charged to land here, unless you are staying in the centre.

19   Kincraig Bridge at end of Loch Insh (NN 835 056; 56.2286, -3.8813). River speeds up. Access right bank below bridge (park in large lay-by opposite church), and access 100m downstream over rough track running parallel with road. As there are nesting ospreys on the island, which are protected by law, please don't land on the island between April and October.

20   Gravel islands where River Feshie enters from right. Nice rapids both above and below this point.

29   Aviemore Bridge (NN 894 116; 56.2839, -3.7886). Access left bank below the old road bridge by the pub, though often crowded. There is a campsite at Coylumbridge, 2km to the right – possible, but a haul if tired! This first stretch of 29km can be paddled in 5–8 hours, making a good first day or half day. From here to Grantown is mainly slow and deep. The section down to Boat of Garten has some good little rapids, but also tree hazards.

40   Boat of Garten Bridge (NN 946 191; 56.3525, -3.7076). Access left bank downstream of road bridge. Island below, good for a stop.

46   After a long, straight stretch, often subject to winds, comes Broomhill Bridge (NN 998 224; 56.3832, -3.6247) – Nethy Bridge village to right. Access left bank. There is a campsite soon, if tired!

47.5 River Dulnain joins from left.

48   Some standing stones appear on left bank, indicating that Boat of Balliefurth campsite is near.

48.5 Boat of Balliefurth on right bank (NJ 013 245; 57.3004, -3.6400). A sign tells you that canoeists are welcome. Camping is on the bank, with a farmyard at the back, with cold water tap, and toilet. Proprietors will come down and take money, and have been very helpful and friendly – their house is some 500m away. This campsite can be a useful distance for a first night's camp if starting from Loch Insh (30km).

52   Grantown road bridge on the A939 (NJ 034 268; 57.3215, -3.6061). Good landing and parking just before bridge on left. Rocks appear in river, warning of the long and interesting Grantown rapid ahead after bridge. It is an easy to inspect grade 2,

The Washing Machine, River Spey   📷 *Pete White*

finishing below the old bridge some 0.5km further down.

56.5 After a pleasant wooded stretch in a deep valley, Cromdale bridge (NJ 066 289; 57.3410, -3.5537), village to right. Access right bank below road bridge, by the church. The next 10 or 11km are fast-flowing, with good scenery.

58.5 Island.

60 Road near on right bank.

61 Dellefure Burn on left, and road. Limited access and parking (NJ 085 316; 57.3656, -3.5231).

64 Islands.

66 Advie Bridge (NJ 120 354; 57.4005, -3.4663), landing and parking on left bank, park on verge opposite 5-bar gate. Pretty wooded stretch with islands follows, shallow in low water. Possible wild campsites in woods after another 2km.

71 Road alongside on left bank, Dalnapot (also known as Ballindalloch). Good parking spots (NJ 158 370; 57.4155, -3.4036) for starting a trip on the faster stretches coming up. The area at Ballindalloch has been cleared to form a good car park off the riverside road. From this spot, a paddle of some 17km down to Aberlour will give any paddler

a very good day trip. This is reached by coming off the A95, over Blacksboat Bridge on the B9138, and turning left up the valley for some 3km. The other Ballindalloch parking place is for those using the Speyside Way campsite, by the old station, right bank – access on left bank just below old railway bridge (NJ 69 369; 57.4148, -3.3853), as below.

71.5 Old railway bridge, long distance footpath goes over it.

72 River Avon (pronounced 'Ayon') joins from right, heralded by far faster water than so far encountered, and a couple of good grade 2 rapids.

73 The first gripping experience for those in open canoes, the rapid known as Blacksboat Rapid, the 'Washing Machine', or various other names. A good grade 2 ramp between shingle banks, with a long wave train. Even in medium flows, this rapid can fill a canoe!

74 Blacksboat Bridge (NJ 184 390; 57.4340, -3.3610). Camping is allowed at the old station on the left (take out above bridge on left), but there are no facilities. Ballindalloch Estate have to be contacted first.

76.5 Fast water down to Knockando (NJ 1904 1416; 57.2110, -3.3422). When bends, a first island, and the old distillery chimney come into sight, you are nearly there. The rapids are not difficult. The middle channel is normally taken, ending in a drop near the left bank. There is landing immediately below, and steps up to the car park. This is an SCA facility, but it is envisaged that touring paddlers will only pass through. In the next 4km are 5 further rapids, all interesting and obvious, large waves in high water down to Carron. Scenic wooded valley.

80.5 Carron Bridge (NJ 225 411; 57.4536, -3.2934). Access left bank by bridge. Now some 3km of good grade 2 rapids.

83.5 The last of the series of rapids with an appreciable drop.

85 Charlestown of Aberlour village to right, footbridge (NJ 262 429; 57.4703, -3.2322), park on right bank, with vehicle access. Shallow stretch to next bridge.

88.5 Craigellachie Bridge, known as Craigel-lachie Old Bridge) followed by new road bridge, with a rapid under it. Access from car park on right bank (NJ 286 451). Just downstream of the rapid on the right bank, is a landing with parking nearby, Boat O'Fiddich. There is a formal campsite is 2.5km away, at the back of Aberlour village. While a very pleasant site, it really requires a vehicle, or a very long and uphill trolley portage. This last 24km to the sea can be completed in a half day. For many kilometres, the bulk of Ben Aigan on the right bank dominates the scenery.

91 The A941 on left bank, parking.

93.5 Rothes to the left, no easy access. After shallow gravel rapids, two sudden drops just before Boat O'Brig.

99 Boat O'Brig road and rail bridges. Access left bank, below road bridge, where there is some parking, reached from the minor road crossing the river (NJ 318 516; 57.5493, -3.1413). The river now unexpectedly enters a scenic stretch with islands, and good stopping places, and the dramatic red sandstone cliffs of the Orton earth pillars (or the 'Seven Pillars of Hercules') on the right bank. There can be sudden winds while under the cliffs.

104 HT power lines cross the river, viewpoint on the cliffs far above. Only 3km to Fochabers.

107 Fochabers village to right, park with access and parking on right bank.

107.5 Fochabers Bridge, A96 trunk road. Access on right, below bridge (NJ 341 596; 57.6215, -3.1050), via a track from the riverside road. The scenery changes again, to a flat, gravelly bed, with many islands. There is still a fast current.

111 It's easy to get lost amongst little gravel runs and islands with shrubs in the summer.

112.5 Disused railway bridge, now used as footbridge. A sign you are nearly at the end!

113.5 Surprisingly, the tidal limit, with the sea at Spey Bay in sight. One of the most unusual estuaries in the UK. Landing on the right bank, to reach the car park, you'll find Moray Firth Wildlife Centre (NJ 349 656; 57.6755, -3.0933), part of the Whales and Dolphin Conservation Society museum, and Tugnet Icehouse. Great mounds of shingle. All facilities to be found at the centre, including a really good café.

114 The open sea. Shallows, sandbanks and channels to the left. There is a campsite next to the Spey Bay Golf Course, near the former hotel.

Note: there is a very short estuary of maybe 200m, and the tides can be ignored, except in a strong onshore wind. Landing can always be made before the tidal limit.

Fun on the Deveron   ◙ *Mike Forrester*

086 River Deveron

Length	50km
OS	29
Grade	2
Tides	Last km, little effect

Portages

Possible portages at Milltown of Rothiemay (400m), and at Marnoch Lodge Bridge (400m).

Introduction

This little-known and charming river gives the paddler nearly 50km, and two days of paddling through the Banff and Buchan countryside, which is quite isolated, being mixed farming and forest, with few facilities. The scenery is mixed, with wooded gorges and small farms, and in high water gives a fast and flat paddle. The last part to the sea is still scenic, with a very short estuary.

Water Level

Look at shallows either near Huntly at the start, or over the bridge at Turriff, to gauge an idea of the depth of water.

Access

The area of the highest start point is reached from the A96 main Aberdeen to Inverness road near Huntly, where the river is first seen (NJ 515 408; 57.4549, -2.8100). In order to avoid rocky shallows, the recommended start point is off the B9188 on left bank (NJ 535 476; 57.5162, -2.7779) where the River Isla joins. As far as Turriff, roads are rarely near the river, but the final section is followed by a minor road on the east bank, and then the A97 near Banff, with the final egress at the road bridge between Banff and Macduff (NJ 695 638; 57.6631, -2.5129).

Campsites & accommodation

There are no formal campsites on the river, the nearest being a caravan site at Turriff. A better bet, if wishing to make a camp base in the area, is to go to the coast to the north.

Description

Km

0   Road on left bank (NJ 535 476; 57.5162, -2.7779). River Isla joins.

1.0 Road comes close to left bank. Inspect next 400m (possible portage on left bank). Small rocky weir, followed by rough water, an island, and further on a broken weir.

1.5 Milltown of Rothiemay Bridge. Picturesque and unspoilt village to left. River bends to right, then a long bend to left, to head north, in deep wooded valley.

9.5 Road on left bank, river heads east.

10.5 Marnoch village on left bank.

12.0 Tight bends to right and then left, 400m of rocky water down to bridge (inspection and possible portage, left bank). Marnoch Lodge Bridge. Access probably on left side. There are no more rapids from here to the sea. Kinnairdy Castle on left bank. River heads south, then east.

16.5 Burn joins from right. Farm roads on both sides, ford. Bend to left, large island, pass on right side.

20.5 Minor road on right bank.

28.0 Major road, B9025 on right bank, approaching Turriff.

29.0 Turriff Bridge, town on hill to right. Rapid under bridge. River slows and meanders, but good current in high water.
There are no more public road bridges between here and Banff.

33.0 Island, take right channel.

37.0 Road on right bank.

44.0 Bridge of Alvah, ancient road bridge – access out on right bank, through private road and farm.

47.0 Woodland walks on left bank, islands. No easy access out to road.

47.5 River becomes tidal.

49.5 Final road bridge, Banff Bay. Banff town to left, MacDuff to right. Egress on left side, upstream of bridge. Very small lay-by here, but parking is better over main road on Bridge Road. (If river is low and tide is out, this last 2km can be problematic due to shallows).

Other important points

The Deveron rises on The Buck, the main peak in the Ladder Hills on the Moray/Aberdeenshire border, and flows north and east towards Huntly. It has been kayaked from Haugh of Glass, off the Dufftown road, 14km down to Huntly, where the river is a bouldery grade 2/3. The 9km further to the confluence with the Isla is still boulder-strewn, with many small weirs, and a start near Milltown of Rothiemay is recommended.

087 River Don 🦦 🏊 ⛺ 🐀

Length	91km
OS	37/38
Grade	1/2

Introduction

The Don rises in the empty mountain area just to the east of the Cairngorm Avon valley, and flows mainly east to the sea. The river is of quite an exceptional length and nearly 100km of this length might be canoeable. Unfortunately it does not carry the same volume of water as its neighbour, the Dee to the south. So, if caught high, the Don gives some delightful paddling through pretty rather than spectacular countryside, but it has to be paddled in times of snow-melt or immediately after heavy rain. In the middle reaches, the river needs to be full, almost to the top of the banks.

River Don and Bennachie 📷 *Mike Forrester*

Water Level
The river should be inspected in the middle or higher stretches. The Don needs a lot of water to be navigable for all its length, often full to the banks, otherwise a great deal of wading may be required.

Access
Distances are given from Glenbuchat (NJ 400 149; 57.2209, -2.9953), but a more sensible start can be made at Glenkindie (NJ 439 138; 57.2115, -2.9305). Alford (NJ 561 172; 57.2434, -2.7291), Pitfichie Castle Bridge (NJ 681 165; 57.2381, -2.5301), recommended egress at Inverurie (NJ 776 206; 57.2755, -2.3731).

Itineraries
Day trips and distances recommended are: Glenkindie to Alford – 21km, Alford to Pitfichie Castle Bridge – 16km, or Pitfichie Castle to Inverurie – 16km.

Campsites & accommodation
The only obvious and active campsite in the whole area is Haughton House and Country Park (NJ 582 170; 57.2418, -2.6942) at Alford, run by Aberdeenshire Council, from which launching is also possible.

Description

Km

0   Glenbuchat Castle left. Water of Buchat joins from left. Valley opens out. Parking on flat ground by river.

2.5   Footbridge.

4.0   Islands, then road bridge, B-road, Glenkindie village on left. Car parking on left.

7.0   Road bridge. Milltown of Towie on left. No easy parking.

11.0   Road bridge, Mill of Brux on right, parking on left.

13.5   Farm bridge.

17.5   Brux footbridge. Steep wooded slopes for next few kilometres. The A944 is present now on left bank – frequent lay-bys for parking. The river can be shallow and rocky.

21.0   Farm bridge and church on left.

26.0   Bridge of Alford. A944. Alford village 2km right. No easy access or egress, busy main road.

28.0   Minor road bridge, Montgarrie village, access possible. Aberdeenshire Council campsite 1km on right in country park. Possible launching from park, 0.5km downstream from this bridge. This is reached by driving right through the caravan park, launching, and then leaving vehicles in car park by Haughton House.

34   Oakbank road bridge. River now enters a wooded gorge, many minor rapids. This bridge is high, but there is access.

35   Weir, followed by footbridge. A further 2km on, a launch point near Glenton would give a nice run through the valley, but parking is difficult.

38.5   Mill of Tilliefoure on left bank. Road on left, footbridge. Best possible launch site for this stretch. Hill on left has many pleasant walks. The river runs in a pretty steep-sided valley, with quite continuous bedrock rapids, between the hills of Scare Hill and Pitfichie.

41 Donview car park (FC) on left, but no access to river.

42.0 Possible parking on bank, at ornamental gates. Broken weir, followed by 0.5km of rapids.

44 Road bridge, river now slows down. Pitfichie Castle on right bank, Monymusk village on right, 2km. The Don is now slow, and meandering, useful for teaching beginners.

50.0 Kemnay, road bridge. Access also from village on right bank, about half a kilometre downstream.

59 Main A96 road bridge (high) at Inverurie. Weir just before this. Egress at next road bridge, Inverurie town to the left.

Other importnt points

Upstream – From Cockbridge, the river is twisty and rocky, but has been paddled in high water. This is easier by kayak than canoe. Just before Strathdon village is a narrow gorge with some fall. After this first 23km there is a car park and toilets at Bellabeg (NJ 353 131; 57.2041, -3.0727), which is the west side of the straggling Strathdon village. This is a convenient start point in high water for experienced paddlers. However, the river is still frequently rocky for the 9km down to Glenbuchat Castle, with a weir just upstream of the first road bridge over the A944. No easy access at either this bridge or the one 2km downstream.

Downstream – It is a further 30km down to the Bridge of Don at Aberdeen. Where the Don enters the outskirts of Aberdeen is the start of

what once was a heavily-industrialised area, with many mills. The use of water power lead to many weirs being constructed, and many of these can give the paddler problems, with broken sluices and difficult or near-impossible portages. The weirs are problems rather than enjoyable challenges, therefore this guide ends at Inverurie, (NJ 776 206; 57.2755, -2.3731). The river can, however, be paddled, taking care to inspect weirs, down to Seaton Park, just before the Bridge of Don in Aberdeen.

088 River Dee

Length	105km
OS	43/44/38
Grade	1/2 (3)

Grade

Grade 1/2 for most of length. There are short grade 3 sections at Linn of Dee, Inverey, Invercauld, Dinnet, and between Potarch and Banchory. Banchory to Aberdeen is grade 1 with short grade 2 sections.

Introduction

The Dee is one of the four big rivers in Scotland, providing long canoe-camping trips, although it tends to carry the least water. It is characterised by long, stony, shallow rapids, but in condition provides beautiful scenery, and like much of the north-east, there is a sense of comparative isolation and little population. This applies especially in the spring and autumn when water levels are likely to be at their best, but an advantage of the north-east climate can be very dry winter trips, with the river still up enough. October is especially recommended, as the autumn colours are at their best, and the fishing season nearly over. The Dee rises on the Lairig Ghru, the major pass

River Dee, near Aboyne 📷 *Eddie Palmer*

in the Cairngorms to the west of Ben Macdui, and reaches the sea at Scotland's third city, Aberdeen.

Note: The large floods in January 2016 changed the river in several ways, with many large rocks in otherwise stony rapids above Dinnet. Tree strainers (potentially very dangerous obstructions – anticipate and avoid!) are now common all the way down the river, as banks collapse over time.

Water Level

For open canoes, the river down to Balmoral can often be quite dry, and a start below here is recommended. The river needs to be obviously up at any of the rapids inspected.

Access

The river valley is conveniently followed by the A93 for most of its length.

Campsites & accommodation

There are, very conveniently, campsites at Braemar, Ballater Aboyne Loch, Banchory, and Maryculter to give a superb 3-day trip, but groups have taken four days, and wild camping is possible in many places. As the valley is open, parking for vehicles near the river is mainly easy.

Short easy trips

Banchory to Maryculter – 17km, and Maryculter to Aberdeen (Aberdeen Boat Club) – 12km.

Description

Km

0   Victoria Bridge, opposite Mar Lodge (4km downstream from Linn of Dee, the highest possible start-point (this whole 6km stretch is grade 2/3). Road comes near

river upstream of bridge. The river is broad and shallow, with shingle. Unfortunately, this upper stretch now has many tree obstacles.

6 Braemar on right. A touristy little town with most facilities, and a campsite to the south, away from the river. Downstream of confluence with the River Clunie, care required for deer fence across river at high water levels; there is gate in the fence on the right if too hazardous to paddle. Access/egress left bank downstream of bridge, river bend, car park on the road.

11.5 Invercauld Bridge. The next part must be inspected, 400m of grade 2/3, depending on height. Awkward rocky passage in an open canoe. River now alongside road (A93), so inspection for water is quite easy.

21.5 Crathie/Balmoral Bridge, rapid under bridge altered by floods, inspection advised. Between here and Ballater, rapid/pool/rapid sequence. After Coilacreich (NO 323 967; 57.0564, -3.1179), river steepens, grade 2 boulder rapids.

32.5 River Gairn joins left. Several rapids on this stretch before Ballater.

35 River Muick joins right - much more water in river after this point.

36 Ballater access/egress point at car park when approaching town (no sign off main road), followed by campsite left, and village. Ballater road bridge, egress on left bank below bridge.
The next section to Dinnet has fast water below Cambus O'May, and rapids before Dinnet.

41 Valley narrows, road and cycle path on left bank. Access. Cambus O'May is the name of the next stretch of fast water.

42 Footbridge, old Victorian suspension bridge, now mostly demolished and dangerous. Access/egress downstream on left after bridge. Parking on left bank. Hotel over the main road.

44 Several rocky rapids, gradually building up.

47 Heavy, rocky rapid and drop before Dinnet Bridge, on left-hand bend. A grade 3 rapid, and more technical in low water. In high water, the route is hard down left side. Egress and inspection best before bridge on right bank, up farm track. Parking on road left side of bridge.

48 Dinnet Bridge. High drop, access awkward. Three sections with islands in next stretch down to Aboyne. River quietens down.

55 Aboyne Bridge. Boat Inn and town to left, egress left below bridge, steep banks.

60 Large islands. River quietens down, stoney rapids.

63 Main road on left bank.

64 Kincardine O'Neil village to left.

67 Potarch Bridge. Large rapid above bridge in high water. Parking on left above bridge. Potarch Hotel on right bank. Start of the very popular run down to Banchory.

68 Lay-by on left bank, access here avoids at least a kilometre of flat water above it. After a bend to the left, small rapids commence.

69 Next 4km regular easy rapids in pretty wooded scenery. Many fishing lodges and croys.

73 At bend to left, river obviously drops more, and is rocky. Cairnton House on left bank. Cairnton Rapid has a first drop

Dinnet Rapid, River Dee © *Eddie Palmer*

which looks awkward, but drops easily into further waves. Inspect left. At the point where the waves finish, a rocky right bank can be seen, and a wooden building the indicator of Invercannie rapid. Inspect on left side.

74 Invercannie rapid drops near right bank, with one large drop, large wave, and breakouts on right, followed in 100m by another rapid down right side. Water-works obvious on left bank. This first drop and wave can swamp an open canoe. The difficulty probably rises to grade 3 in high water, but open canoes usually shoot this with no bother.

About 500m downstream, Mill Drop on right, big boulders and wave train, grade 2. Several grade 2 long bouldery rapids down to Banchory.

76.5 Banchory Bridge. Access left bank above bridge, campsite on left below bridge. Parking options up the road to the left.

About 600m downstream, River Feugh joins from right. Hotel on left bank, and a fast grade 2 rapid with waves, and a boulder left bank.

Easy grade 1 rapids from now on.

82 Durris Bridge, Crathes to left. Egress on right below bridge, small parking area.

87 Keiths Muir or Drumoak Bridge, now closed to road traffic, and access to river very awkward. Islands with many trees, on banks, and in river.

93.5 Maryculter Bridge. Peterculter village left. Egress left by path below church.

95 Twin road bridges, B979 and new Aberdeen by-pass bridge. Lay-by on B979 100m north of bridge. Valley now feeling more built up.

96 Island on righthand bend, left channel the best, the right channel tree-choked.

100 Shakkin' Briggie, abandoned footbridge

103 Bridge of Dee. Tidal limit. Aberdeen city limits. Access left bank next to fishing hut

104 Road bridge.

105 Railway bridge.

105.5 Pedestrian footbridge, and road bridge, followed by Aberdeen Boat Club boathouse on right bank. Egress at rowing club steps. Compulsory egress, due to Aberdeen Harbour Regulations.

Tayside

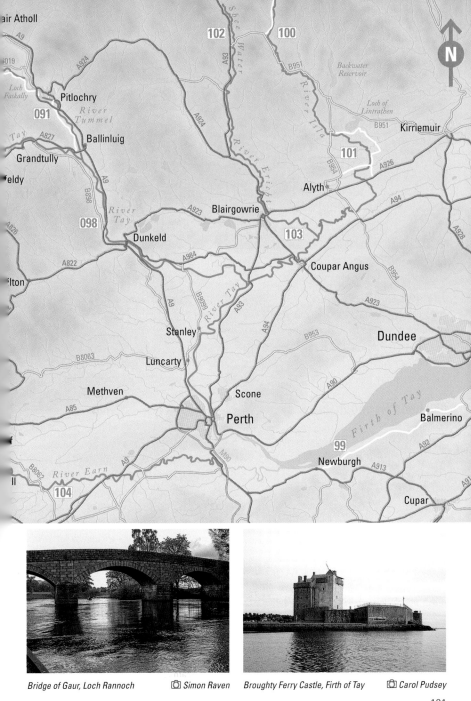

Bridge of Gaur, Loch Rannoch   📷 *Simon Raven*   *Broughty Ferry Castle, Firth of Tay*   📷 *Carol Pudsey*

Loch Rannoch
📷 Pete White

Tayside

The Tay catchment is one of the largest, if not the largest, in Scotland, and a long touring trip can be planned, using either the Dochart, Loch Tay and River Tay route, or the Rannoch, Tummel and Tay valleys.

089 Loch Rannoch

Length	Round trip of up to 30km
OS	42

Introduction

A loch with a wild feel, but also quite close to civilisation.

Access

Loch Rannoch can be accessed either at Bridge of Gaur (NN 501 567; 56.6779, -4.4495), at its western end, or from the B846 on the north shore (NN 51 57; 56.6809, -4.4350), a few kilometres east, or near Kinloch Rannoch at the eastern end, where the road nears the loch, and has parking (NN 659 578; 56.6926, -4.1921).

Campsites & accommodation

Tummel Bridge to the east.

Description

The loch is 15km long, with relatively few places to egress, but there are plenty of stopping places. It is a favourite second home area for Scots from the central belt, and has almost a Canadian feel with its surrounding wooded mountains.

At the eastern end is a weir within a sluice gate, which can be carried around on the left, or a landing made on the right side some 100m away. This is followed by the road bridge carrying a minor road over to Aberfeldy to the south. Kinloch Rannoch village to left, with hotels etc, and a community café and post office.

2.5km of river carry the paddler down to Dunalastair Loch, with islands and trees, and then a 1.5km narrow stretch to the dam. Egress now needs to be before the narrowing on the loch, on to the road, left side, via a vague track (NN 708 586; 56.7012, -4.1125).

North shore of Loch Tummel *Carol Pudsey*

Clunie Dam, Loch Tummel *Carol Pudsey*

Short easy trips
Kinloch Rannoch to west – various trips, of up to 30km or as short as you like.

Other important points
In days gone by, canoes were portaged down the road on the left bank to Loch Tummel, but this is not now possible due to gaps in the boundary fences now being blocked.

090 Loch Tummel

Length	Round trip of up to 22km
OS	43/52

Introduction
A loch with more of a 'closed-in' feel than Rannoch, as it is narrower, and much more wooded.

Access
The B8019 runs along the north side, but physical access is not easy. It is better from Tummel Bridge, south side (NN 76 59; 56.7062, -4.0277), the sailing club, south side (NN 798 587; 56.7045, -3.9655), or near the Clunie Dam at the east end (NN 884 602; 56.7201, -3.8256) on the south shore (some parking). Unfortunately, due to an increase in 'dirty informal camping', access on to Loch Tummel is now far more difficult, with camping being discouraged.

Campsites & accommodation
At Tummel Bridge, Queen's View on the north side, or at Pitlochry to the east.

Description
The loch is 11km long, with a sailing club on the south shore, and roads on both banks. Near the eastern end is Queen's View, a viewpoint and visitor centre, with camp and caravan site. The loch is quite narrow just west of Queen's View, with wooded islands.

091 Lower River Tummel

Length	9.5km
OS	52
Grade	1/2

Introduction
The lower section of the River Tummel flows out of Loch Faskally at Pitlochry for over 6km to join the Tay, and is a pleasant short paddle. It could be added to a trip on the Tay down to Dunkeld

Pitlochry dam and Festival Theatre, Lower River Tummel　　　　　　　　　　*Janet Moxley*

Water Level
The Tummel relies on dam releases (information on SCA website), and is often dry in summer. It is usually very shallow and stony. Inspection from the A9 bridge over the river on the Pitlochry by-pass will tell you if there looks to be enough water.

Access
Near the top end of Faskally Reservoir, access is from the A road leading off the former A9 road, now the B8019 to Killiekrankie and Blair Atholl. A road leaves left off this B-road, when heading north to 'Forest Walks', and a research laboratory, with access on to the lake at NN 920 597; 56.7165, -3.7666. Egress is at Ballinluig Bridge, east side, on to minor road, with parking (NN 976 521; 56.6495, -3.6720).

Campsites & accommodation
In and around Pitlochry (three large sites).

Description
It is 3km down to the dam and fish ladders at Pitlochry. The portage around the dam is best made on the west side, around awkward corners on a path. To avoid the long portage at Pitlochry Dam an easier trip can be had from a road below the dam running from the parking area for Pitlochry Theatre.

It is a flat and stony grade 1 and grade 2 for 6.5km down to the junction with the Tay below Ballinluig.

Other important points
Just above the described launch point, the River Garry joins from the Killiecrankie Pass. An alternative start would be to launch on to the Garry at the Garry Bridge 1km upstream.

092 Loch Daimh

Length	Round trip of up to 12km
OS	51

Introduction
This isolated loch stands in a wild and bare landscape amongst mountains.

Access
Approached either by the very long road up Glen Lyon from Aberfeldy and Fortingall, or by the fairly new road from the south, via Killin

and Glen Lochay, to the unsignposted turn off to the loch (NN 538 457; 56.5804, -4.3829), and 3km up to the dam. It is a reservoir for Scottish and Southern Energy, and the road has ample parking at its end for both walkers and anglers. From the end of the road, at a locked gate (NN 510 464; 56.5858, -4.4289), it is a stiff climb up the height of the dam with a canoe or kayak.

Campsites & accommodation

There are none in Glen Lyon. The nearest is at either Killin or Aberfeldy.

Description

The loch is some 6km long, offering the possibility of lovely wild camping at its head. There are a number of small islands, including four that only appear at low water levels when the loch is drawn down.

093 Loch Lyon

Length	Round trip of up to 16km
OS	51

Introduction

Loch Lyon is similar to Loch Daimh in landscape, being at the end of the longest glen road in Scotland, some 35km long.

Access

From the road up Glen Lyon from Aberfeldy and Fortingall, or over the hills from the south from Killin, to the dam (NN 460 420; 56.5447, -4.5077). The public road finishes at Pubil, a kilometre before the dam. A farm track continues up to the loch, and if gates are open may give the paddler road access on to the water. Otherwise, it is a case of carrying boats.

Campsites & accommodation

There are none in Glen Lyon. The nearest is at either Killin or Aberfeldy.

Description

The mountains to the west form the boundary between Perthshire and Highland (Glen Orchy). There are two interesting arms of the loch, to the north-west and south-west at the west end, the latter giving a total length for paddling of some 8km. This south-west branch is perhaps the most interesting for landing and camping as the north-west one has more farming activity.

094 Upper River Lyon

Length	12km
OS	51
Grade	1–2

Introduction

The described section of the River Lyon is delightful and easy, turning from a wide open, peaceful valley to a narrower and wooded one downstream.

Water Level

Obvious at the start – the shingle rapids need to be covered.

Access

Bridge of Balgie (NN 577 468; 56.5915, -4.3200). Egress is near Chesthill, where the road is alongside the river (NN 690 473; 56.5992, -4.1361), well before the obvious rocky gorge downstream.

Campsites & accommodation

None local. The nearest are at Aberfeldy or Killin.

Description

From Bridge of Balgie it is a gentle 11km grade 1 paddle down to where the river narrows and increases in difficulty. The rapid under the bridge that marks the start of this section can be easily inspected and portaged if required. The egress comes just after a footbridge where the road is alongside the river.

Other important points

There are hard white-water sections upstream and downstream (see *Scottish White Water*).

095 Lower River Lyon

Length	6km
OS	51
Grade	1(2–3)

Introduction

The Lower Lyon as described here runs from Bridge of Lyon (the take-out for the whitewater section upstream) down to the bridge near Keltneyburn, where the Kenmore road leaves the B846. This 6 stretch is both lovely, and an ideal introduction to an interesting grade 2-3 rapid. The rest is grade 1.

Water Level

The rapid downstream of Bridge of Lyon needs to be covered.

Access

The start at Bridge of Lyon (NN 729 467; 56.5949, -4.0723) has very scarce parking, the egress at Comrie Castle (NN 786 488; 56.6153, -3.9804) has a lay-by next to the river, downstream of the bridge, river left.

Campsites & accommodation

Aberfeldy.

Description

There are no difficulties, apart from near the end, when pylons are clearly visible, and the river narrows. A first minor drop leads round a corner to the right, the second drop has a definite fall on the right side of river, and a couple more small drops follow, between rocks. The pylon line crosses the river halfway down a 400m stretch of rapids. Portaging this is quite difficult, on the right bank. After a flat pool there is a second shallow stretch, but no drops. At the end of this, the Keltneyburn joins on the left and it is another 1.3km to the take out at the road brige.

Other important points

The trip from Bridge of Lyon down to the Tay, and on to Aberfeldy is an ideal day trip if the water is high enough. The best way to judge this is downstream from Bridge of Lyon. If the shingle is well-covered, the river is high enough.

096 River Fillan and River Dochart

Length	21.5km
OS	50/51
Grade	2–3

Portages

Two possible portages, at Corriechaorach (NN 466 281; 56.4201, -4.4898) and Lix rapids (NN 550 311; 56.4497, -4.3552).

Introduction

This river gives a nice paddling introduction to

Lower River Tummel   📷 *Janet Moxley*

the Tay catchment, the Dochart being a pretty river with a couple of good rapids (grade 2–3). The valley is many people's introduction to the West Highlands, as they drive up the A82 through Crianlarich and Tyndrum.

Water Level

At the Lix rapids, visual inspection should show that they are easily paddled.

Access

From the A82, access at Crianlarich railway bridge (NN 385 255; 56.3941, -4.6195). There is a village store, Post Office, and railway station nearby. (When I was looking at this site again, an elderly man came up to me, and said that he remembered canoeists coming here before WW2, he thought in 1938. They were from England, had of course come by train, and they trolleyed their soft-skinned kayaks and gear down from the railway station, and camped beside the river. The man envied them (he was about 20 then), but he never took up canoeing! Egress above the Falls of Dochart (NN 563 318; 56.4564, -4.3345). A minor road

follows the north bank down the lower stretch, useful for inspecting the Lix rapids.

Campsites & accommodation

At Tyndrum, Killin, and on Loch Tay.

Description

Km

0   Crianlarich railway bridge. Access down a grass track, just downstream of the bridge over the A85, on north side. No camping allowed, but parking is good on that side of the main road. The River Fillan is absolutely flat down to the loch, and is like a canal.

2   The river enters Loch Dochart – islands and castle on upper loch, short section of river to Loch lubhair.

5   Parking and picnic site off A85, a very convenient place to start.

6   The loch gradually starts to move, and becomes the River Dochart. Wooded and pretty.

7   Private road bridge to Loch Dochart estate and house.

8   Road bridge to Auchessan Farm, much used by walkers and climbers. Minor rocky rapids.

10.5 Rapid at Corriechaorach starts on left, moves over to centre. Quite shootable in open canoe with care. Inspect from river left, not easy to portage left.

12   Bridge over to Inishewan. River meanders a bit more, islands.

14.5 Auchlyne road bridge. Some parking, and access on to river. River now slows right down as far as the Lix rapids. Meanders over a flat plain. B-road on left bank.

20   Woodland starts on right bank, giving warning of the approaching rapids, which start immediately where left bank is wooded, and road is right alongside. Lix Toll junction on A85 is on right bank, 1km. Two main drops, followed by a rocky stretch over some 500m. Not difficult with good steering. Bottom of rapids is a good place to take out, unless intending to also do the Falls of Dochart (usually graded 4 plus, and for many years thought to be uncanoeable).

21.5 Lay-by on B-road (river left), last take-out (NN 563 318; 56.4564, -4.3345) before Falls of Dochart!

Other important points

The upper river – the river initially rises in the corrie of Ben Lui, a spectacular Munroe to the south of Tyndrum, and is known as the Cononish until the bridge at Dalrigh (SW), which was on the old road. This upper river is hardly navigable by kayaks. It then becomes the Fillan, and flows the 5km down the flat valley to Crianlarich, and a further 2km to Loch Dochart. Access and egress on this stretch is only by private roads to houses or campsites.

097 Loch Tay

Length   Round trip of up to 48km
OS   51

Introduction

Loch Tay is some 24km long, running to the north-east from Killin to the end at Kenmore, where the River Tay leaves. The scenery is fine, and very different from what you see from the road along the north side.

Access

Access to the loch is usually from the Killin Hotel car park (NN 573 334; 56.4711, -4.3191) on to the short River Lochay; permission should be asked for this, and vehicles removed after access. The A827 follows the north side of the loch, but not very often near the water. There is also access/egress at Fearnan (NN 715 443; 56.5730, -4.0939), and at Kenmore, several places near the watersports centre and car park (NN 77 45; 56.5808, -4.0047).

Campsites & accommodation

At Killin and Kenmore.

Description

The loch is worth a 2-day trip with camping. A short day's paddle would bring you to the woodland, and waterfall 19km along, opposite Ardreonaig on the south shore (outdoor centre here). Camping possible here. Along most of the loch the roads and human habitation are not very visible. The road comes alongside on the north side near Fearnan after 18km (outdoor centre here also).

Kenmore provides a castle, two crannogs (iron age lake dwellings), a watersports centre, car parking, two hotels, and the entrance to the Tay, with a camp and caravan site on the left.

Reconstructed Crannog on Loch Tay   📷 *Colin Anderson*

Short easy trips
From Killin at the east end of the loch, there and back trips from as short as you like up to 20km.

Other important points
1. It is also possible to start the trip from further up the River Lochay. This gives some 4km of paddling, down from a road bridge below a fall (but often low in water).
2. When combined with the River Tay, this is a possible 5-day trip with usually reliable water, and great scenery.

098 River Tay

Length	75km
OS	51/52/53
Grade	1/2 (2–3) (3)

Grade
Grade 1/2, except Grandtully and Stanley, both grade 3 and a few grade 2–3 rapids described below.

Portages
Both Grandtully and Stanley can be avoided, the former by a portage down the right bank just downstream of the house, the latter by a portage, and using a mill lade.

Introduction
The Tay is another Scottish classic, keeping its level much better than other long rivers due to its massive catchment area, the existence of Loch Tay, and its headwaters being virtually on the wet west coast. The river gives 75km of paddling, usually without any portage or wading. There are two famous stretches of white water, Grandtully and the Stanley stretch, which can be coped with by the bold (see also *Scottish White Water*). The rest are easy grade 2 rapids.

Communication is easy up the Tay valley, with the A9 and A827 near for most of the way, so vehicle shuttles are straightforward.

Water Level
The Tay can be paddled in almost any water, and for much of the year tends to be high when other rivers have lost their water. A look at the river at Grandtully from the bank gives a good idea of level, as does the SEPA gauge (Where's the Water, SCA website).

River Tay   📷 *Eddie Palmer*

Access

Kenmore (NN 772 456; 56.5862, -4.0017),
Aberfeldy (NN 851 494; 56.6223, -3.8747),
Edradynate – SCA Access Point (NN 888 518;
56.6448, -3.8154),
Grandtully (NN 911 531; 56.6570, -3.7785),
Logierait (NN 969 519; 56.6475, -3.6834),
Dunkeld (NO 027 425; 56.5643, -3.5852),
Caputh (NO 089 394; 56.5377, -3.4832),
Kinclaven (Isla Bridge, NO 163 382; 56.5283,
-3.3625),
Stanley (NO 119 338; 56.4880, -3.4325),
Luncarty (NO 101 300; 56.4536, -3.4605),
Waulkmill (NO 106 290; 56.4447, -3.4520).
Final egress in:
Perth (NO 119 240; 56.4000, -3.4292), (NO 120
225; 56.3866, -3.4271) or
Willowgate Centre, (NO 137 218; 56.3806,
-3.3993).

Campsites & accommodation

The upper valley, from Kenmore to Logierait,
has very few 'wild' campsites – most of the
time you would be camping in someone's

back garden. Please use the formal campsite
at Grandtully. There are also campsites at
Kenmore, Aberfeldy, Grandtully, Pitlochry (off
the route), Birnam, and at Perth Racecourse.

Short easy trips

Ballinluig (on River Tummel), down to Dunkeld
– 8km, and Luncarty to Perth – 8km.

Description

Km

0   Kenmore – access on left bank.

2   Chinese Bridge – a very long rapid, which
often catches out paddlers, especially
open canoes. Land on right bank just upstream of the obvious bridge, and before
it to inspect if not sure of route.

3   Footbridge. Large island below, left channel, small islands, right channel.

4   River Lyon joins left – shingle rapid, much
greater flow. (This lower part of the Lyon
is paddleable from below the serious
stretch for some 8km from Bridge of Lyon
to the confluence, see Lower Lyon.)

9 Island, channel down left side but leads on to bank.

10 Aberfeldy in sight, wooded. Footpath on right bank.

10.5 General Wade's Bridge, Aberfeldy, high stone bridge. Good access and egress on right bank, parking on road. Start of 'warm-up' paddle for WW course. Campsite on east side of town. The river meanders around Aberfeldy, with golf course and footbridge.

12.5 Distillery and main road on right. The slalom site for Breadalbane Canoe club is on the right bank

15.5 End of several bends in river, minor road on left bank, start of White Water Race Course – river goes right; long, bouncy rapid, large waves.

16 Edradynate access (SCA) on left bank through field, with parking. (This signed access point is some 3km upriver from Strathtay, on minor road.) Ideal point for a trip down the WW course, through Grandtully. Several good grade 2 rapids follow.

19 Bend to left, and shallow, Grandtully comes into view, and the metal lattice road bridge can be seen. River speeds up, landing is on right hand side just downstream of the house and above main rapids if required. Please do not land on the garden of this house, or paddle down the mill lade in front of it. Slalom wires and poles signify start of lead-in to rapids.

19.5 Plenty of open canoes do Grandtully (grade 3). Inspection from both banks is easy, either downstream of the house on the right hand side or even better, upstream of gabion baskets on the left.

Except for high water, it is easiest to inspect the 'top fall' from the left bank. It is usually shot on left side, fast water to central rock, keep right, and then after the bridge there is a 'lower fall' which is heavy. Grandtully has multiple café/bars, parking at the SCA campsite, a raft operator, and plenty of activity, as it is one of the top kayaking sites in Scotland. Egress below bottom fall on right side. If you are leaving a vehicle at Grandtully for a shuttle, inspection of your chosen egress before you head up the river is highly recommended. Parking for the village is courtesy of the SCA at the campsite on the opposite side of the road from the river.

20.5 A827 road bridge. Islands and shallows just below, narrow channels.

25.5 Old Logierait railway bridge, now used by cyclists, walkers and cars. Wood cabins for hire on left. Road to Ballinluig and A9.

27 River Tummel enters from left. River is now near A9 until Dunkeld.

34.5 A9 road bridge. River through to Dunkeld very attractive, beech woods.

37.5 River Braan joins on right.

38 Dunkeld Bridge. Small town, historic cathedral, shops, café, pubs etc. Town is on the left. Left side of bridge is best, shallow rapid below.

38.5 Birnam village is on the right bank. At sandy beach is the 'big tree' (unofficial) campsite and picnic stop, at back of housing estate. Hills and woods close in.

47 Caputh Bridge, egress on left below bridge.

50.5 River now changes character, with large shingle islands and banks, and a twisting course. Paradise for many bird species.

52 One of the largest Roman camps ever found in Scotland is 0.5km left.

56 Kinclaven Bridge. The River Isla joins the Tay 200m after the bridge. Parking is some 500m river left at the Meikleour Beech Hedge on the main road. It is possible to carry boats over the fence and down to the River Isla, about 300m, and a short paddle takes one on to the Tay. It is also possible to paddle up to here to egress.

57.5 Disused railway bridge. Occasional easy rapids

62.5 The appearance of islands signals the top of the infamous Campsie Linn, a shock of a rapid after miles of nearly flat water. There are four shoots, with rocky and vegetated islands in between. The easiest in normal water is the second from the right, a straightforward drop. In very high water the extreme right through trees is possible. The brave might want to shoot the left route.

Note: For the following stretch of river, you are advised to look at the SCA website details of what might be physical access/egress to the Tay. This is the most heavily paddled piece of water in Scotland. It is desired not to make parking and access to the river a problem for local people.

63 Burnmouth Ferry – car parking by the river, right side. This is reached via the Linn Road from Stanley village – take signs off main road in centre of village to Stanley Mills, and turn left, and then a right turn into Linn Road in an estate of houses. Currently (2020), the locked car park can be accessed by paddlers belonging to one of the UK governing bodies contacting the SCA for the padlock code. The next three miles or so is very heavily fished in spring and autumn – avoid both bank anglers, and what could be many

Thistlebrig Rapid, River Tay   📷 *Eddie Palmer*

fishing boats in the middle of the river.

63.5 Stanley Weir. Three shoots in low to medium water, middle the most water, left easiest. In high water, there is a strong stopper right across the river. Below there is a series of rapids: Catspaws and Hellhole, leading down to a bend to Red Wall, on the left (all grade 2–3). New piles of stones keep appearing in the river due to angling interests.

64 Bend to right – rapid (Fisherman's Bend) deep on right side, shallow to left.

65 Old weir – shallows on right, wall on left, and mill lade. The lade is a beautiful paddle, newly restored in 2004, all the way down to the end of Thistlebrig Rapid. If wishing to take this, go left well upriver, and keep to left bank. The lade has trees across, but is a very pleasant alternative. It has a good current, and is another world altogether. Exit the lade when it starts to bend to the left, obvious steps down to the river. On the river the route is centre of left side. Large holes follow. Restored Stanley Mills on right bank, well worth a visit, has a café. This is a possible alternative launch site if wishing to avoid the rapids upstream. Use the car park, and carry boats to the grassy river bank just

Friarton Bridge, Firth of Tay   ○ *Carol Pudsey*

downstream. Do not park and unload on the access road. River bends to left.

65.5 Thistlebrig Rapid starts, (grade 2–3) centre over to left side, in high water right side possible.

66 Egress on right bank, but very steep walk up (the '39 Steps') to lay-by on B9099 road. Easier egress either at Luncarty or Waulkmill, further downstream.

68 Luncarty on right bank. Access through new housing estate to river, ending in a cul-de-sac and a riverside path with limited parking. A short walk, and canoeists' steps down to river.

69 Waulkmill on left bank. Some car parking.

72 River Almond joins right. River becomes tidal just below here.

75 North Inch, Perth (public park) on right. Parking and landing.

Other important points
Eurasian beavers have spread from an original pair in the River Earn, escapees from a private collection. Feeding signs can be seen in many places on the river, especially amongst willow.

099 Firth of Tay

Length	38km
OS	53/58/54
Tides	Strong tidal streams

Tides and weather
The Tay has the fastest tides of any estuary in the UK. There is absolutely no chance of paddling against it, so obtaining and understanding tide tables is paramount. Many people in small boats have drowned in or on the Tay due to not treating the estuary with respect, underestimating the weather and their abilities, and not planning trips properly.

Introduction
A great trip using the ebb tide all the way down, and a good introduction to estuary paddling.
The estuary is peaceful and very rural for much of the way, with rich bird life. The main channel is buoyed and lit, and small coasters still call at Perth harbour. Beware meeting them at high tide.

Access
Access on at Perth:

North Inch (NO 119 240; 56.4000, -3.4292),
Perth pontoon (NO 121 230; 56.3911, -3.4256).
Then:
Willowgate Centre (NO 137 218; 56.3806, -3.3993),
Inchyra (NO 183 203; 56.3679, -3.3244),
Newburgh (NO 235 185; 56.3526, -3.2396),
Balmerino (NO 357 249; 56.4119, -3.0438),
Newport jetty (NO 419 278; 56.4388, -2.9439),
Egress at:
Tayport harbour (NO 459 290; 56.4500, -2.8793).

Seasonal blockage, Upper Isla   📷 *Eddie Palmer*

Campsites & accommodation
Perth and Monifieth.

Description
Km
0   North Inch, followed by road bridge.
0.5   Road bridge.
1   Railway bridge – river divides, most water on right. Access probably best below here, on west (right) side alongside the South Inch, Perth pontoon (NO 121 230). This is a new Council-provided pontoon, and near parking on the South Inch.
3   Friarton Bridge, carrying the main A90 to Dundee. Willowgate Centre on left bank.
6.5   Elcho Castle to right. Old wharf and landing. Path off river.
8.5   Inchyra village on the left. Small jetty and landing. Sailing club. Small village.
9.5   Pylons cross, very high up. Good landmark.
11   River Earn joins right. Cairnie Pier on left bank gives egress.
12   Buoyed channel for shipping. On right bank are the remains of a Roman camp, and evidence that the Romans built a pontoon bridge across the Tay at this point (only discovered fairly recently).

12.5   Mugdrum Island splits the river. Mugdrum is farmed (though flooded most winters). Farm machinery is taken over for the season by landing craft. The main channel is down right of the island, the left has more mudflats and reed banks (cultivated). The banks down the left side change each winter.
14   Newburgh on right bank. Small town with landing and very friendly sailing club. Was a port years ago. The estuary after this point widens out, with little habitation for quite a distance. Main channel is on the right (south) side.
16.5. Port Allan (small harbour and shelter) on left bank, often hidden behind a reed bank.
18.5   Ballinbreich Castle on right bank.
21   Flisk Point to right – house.
26   Balmerino right – village and landing.
30   Railway bridge – Wormit village on right. Slipway after bridge.
33.5   The 'new' road bridge. Aim for the arches with the navigation lights.
37   Keeping to right bank, Tayport harbour.
38   Crossing over the tideway, Broughty Ferry on left bank, landing by the castle, lowest suggested egress. Royal Tay Yacht Club on left just before Broughty Ferry.

100 Upper River Isla

Length	22.5km
OS	43/44/53
Grade	1–2

Introduction

The Isla is a long and shallow river, with an upper stretch which is easy for kayaks, but a bit more testing for open canoes, a very difficult section in a gorge to by-pass, and then a much flatter part as the river reaches Strathmore. The glen is an attractive one, with the Caenlochan Nature Reserve at its head, the river running off the western slopes of Glas Maol in the Glenshee ski area. This area is a good one for seeing and hearing rutting stags in the autumn. The whole of the upper glen is open, with good views. The only habitation in the glen is the tiny Glenisla village, with a hotel of some reputation for food and good beer.

Water Level

Look at rocky stretch through Glenisla village – if too dry, the river is not worth doing.

Access

From the main road up Glen Isla, the B951. Access at:
Auchavan (NO 192 696; 56.8109, -3.3252) or more usually Little Forter (NO 187 649; 56.7686, -3.3319)
Brewlands Bridge (NO 195 615; 56.7382, -3.3177),
Glenisla village (NO 212 603; 56.7277, -3.2896),
Egress at:
Bridge of Craigisla (NO 252 539; 56.6709, -3.2223).

Campsites & accommodation

Nether Craig, near the egress.

Description

Km

0   In high water, the river can be done by kayak from Auchavan, where the public road ends in the upper glen. Parking for cars, many walkers here. The valley is flat-bottomed, and the river stony and shallow. River follows the road down.

5   Little Forter Bridge. Alternative start here, more water. Just above the bridge there is a slightly more difficult drop over rock slabs. Not much parking here.

9.5   Brewlands Bridge. Parking on grass verges. Old bridge just downstream.

11   Just when buildings in Glenisla village come into sight, the river steepens and becomes more bouldery. Easy for kayaks, more challenging for open canoes, but possible with skill. Nice stretch past the village, constant avoidance of rocks. If landing, stop at village hall and car park at top of village.

13   Old ford, former pub on left bank.

15   Road leaves river, and rapids quieten down. Isla is flat and fairly fast after this. Two left-hand bends with easy drops, where the river appears to be girding up for more, but doesn't. River meanders.

17.5   As the river turns right, with a high slope on the left bank, rapids commence for a constant kilometre.

20   Farm bridge, woods close in on this stretch.

21   Approaching the gorge below, river drops more, with rocky rapids.

22   Old broken weir, now a rapid, route down left of centre. Bends.

22.5 Approaching Bridge of Craigisla, rapids under, ensure swift exit on left, just after bridge, on to parking area.

Other important points

Reekie Linn, the highest waterfall in this part of Scotland, is about 200m downstream of the egress, well worth going to see. A very deep gorge then runs southwards for 6km.

Lower Isla, near Coupar Angus 📷 *Carol Pudsey*

101 Lower River Isla

Length	29.5km
OS	53
Grade	1–2(3)

Portages

Ruthven Falls (grade 3) is an awkward portage and inspection, but can be carried over on the right bank; the left bank is private garden.

Introduction

This section of the Isla runs through the lower valley joining the Tay at Kinclaven. The first part is pleasant wooded countryside, the lower stretches have rather high banks. The lower part of the section described is popular for training and instruction.

Water Level

The river is mainly flat in the lower reaches. At the start, look downstream from the bridge at shallow rapids; if they are covered the river level is high enough.

Access

Airlie Bridge (NO 296 505; 56.6410, -3.1496), Bridge of Ruthven, though very steep access down banks (NO 290 490; 56.6274, -3.1590),

Bridge of Crathies (NO 279 455; 56.5958, -3.1759), Grange of Aberbothrie Bridge (NO 242 447; 56.5881, -3.2359), Couttie's Bridge (NO 211 408; 56.5525, -3.2852), and egress at Bridge of Isla (NO 163 382; 56.5283, -3.3625).

Campsites & accommodation

Nether Craig, (near Craigisla Bridge and Reekie Linn waterfall), Alyth and Blairgowrie.

Short easy trip

Bridge of Crathies, Meigle to Aberbothrie Bridge – 6km.

Description

Km

0 Bridge over gorge on minor road from Airlie to Alyth – spectacular views and vegetation. Access is reasonably easy down steep bank on west side, downstream. Parking for only two vehicles. Small rapids.

2.5 Alyth Burn joins right. Pretty, wooded banks. River starts to steepen and narrow.

4 Mini-gorge, church high on right bank.

4.5 Ruthven Bridge, egress here is awkward. 200m further on, horizon line of Ruthven Falls, old mill on left bank. The falls appear a bit more frightening than they really are, there is a line just right of centre, heading obviously left when over the first drop. Inspection / portage river right. (The falls can be inspected beforehand from a car park on the right bank, but this is not encouraged by local residents, signposted down a small road just west of Ruthven Bridge.) River now flattens out considerably, with wooded banks, and plenty of bird life.

6   River turns 90° to the right.

7   A line of pylons crosses the river, and 500m to the right is the famous 'square-top pylon', where two lines join, and where ospreys have nested for years. Their nest is the untidy jumble, totally unreachable by any predator.

8.5   The Dean Water joins from left (see Angus section). This stretch is often flooded way above the banks in winter.

9   Bridge of Crathies. Parking just north of bridge, also used by anglers. The next stretch is often very congested in the spring by trees and branches after winter floods. The river now winds considerably across Strathmore, and is an ideal piece of easy water for beginners, although not much scenery due to high banks.

15   Aberbothrie Bridge, standing out in the flat countryside. The road can often be flooded in winter. Parking on verges.

17.5   River Ericht joins right (see route 097). This area appears isolated due to lack of roads.

22   Couttie's Bridge, Coupar Angus on obvious hill to left. Access on left bank, grass track up to road, with gate, parking for a maximum of three vehicles. Also used by anglers. Two enormous bends follow, and these open stretches often affected by high winds.

26   Pleasant wooded stretch to left, good stopping place.

29.5   Bridge of Isla. Egress the river on the right bank. Walk about 300m to the right, and over a fence and minor road, to parking at the Meikleour Beech Hedge. The Isla joins the Tay in about 400m.

Shee Water / Ericht

Sections 096 and 097, separated by a harder white water section, are all one river. The Shee Water is formed at Spittal of Glenshee by the junction of three burns. Below these two sections it mysteriously morphs into the Blackwater (grade 4, see *Scottish White Water*) at some point, and then at Bridge of Cally it is joined by the Ardle to become the Ericht, which eventually flows into the Isla.

102 Upper Shee Water

Length	13.5km
OS	43/53
Grade	1–2 (3)

Grade

Grade 1–2, grade 3 at Blacklunans Falls (can be portaged).

Introduction

The Shee Water is set between the spectacular mountains of the Glen Shee ski area, and so even a spring trip can be between snow-clad peaks. Most traffic is heading up north to the main ski area, and not stopping, so a trip on quite an easy river can be done in relative peace and quiet. Due to the U-shaped glaciated valley bottom, the river is flat, and the paddler can enjoy the scenery.

Water Level

Due to a glaciated flat-bottomed valley, the Shee Water, with a high enough flow, can be paddled even by open canoe from the start. This trip does require winter high water.

Access

The A93 runs south to north up the whole glen, passing through Spittal of Glenshee, access (NO 111 699; 56.8121, -3.4580), and Dalrulzion at the finish, egress (NO 136 586; 56.7111, -3.4132).

Campsites & accommodation

In the summer, the campsite at the finish is open. Plenty of accommodation in the glen.

Description

Km

0   Road bridge on A93 (The Blairgowrie to Braemar road, which passes over Glenshee ski area).

2   Private road bridge.

3   Private road bridge.

4.5 Private road bridge – main road nearby.

6.5 Wooded stretch.

8.5 Cray road bridge – parking and launching alongside road below bridge.

11.5 Rocky rapids when road is alongside on left. Egress here, and fall is best inspected.

12 Large fall under Blacklunans Bridge, easier in high water – aim right to avoid rocks below.

13 Three falls, or man-made weirs, heavy in high water. Portage river right. Back garden of former hotel on main road.

13.5 Bridge into campsite. Take out below bridge on left side. (Don't miss as there are falls downstream and no egress before them.)

River Earn and the Braes of Abernethy *Carol Pudsey*

103 Lower Ericht

Length	13km
OS	53
Grade	1

Introduction

A pleasant and gentle paddle through lowland scenery, to join the very meandering River Isla.

Water Level

Look downstream from the bridge in the middle of Blairgowrie – the river should have an obvious route through the shallows downstream with most of the rocks covered.

Access

At Blairgowrie, below the main road bridge (NO 181 450; 56.5897, -3.3354), egress off the Isla at Couttie's Bridge near Coupar Angus (NO 211 408; 56.5525, -3.2852).

Campsites & accommodation

Blairgowrie.

Description

Km

0   In Blairgowrie, take the side road downstream of bridge, right side, which leads to an industrial estate. Launch from side

of the road. River is at first tree-lined, with islands, and pleasant.

6 Increasingly, flood banks block out the view. Flat agricultural countryside.

7.5 Junction with River Isla.

13 Take out at Couttie's Bridge.

104 River Earn

Length	61km (66.5km possible)
OS	51/52/58
Grade	1–2(3)
Tides	Estuary dries out

Grade

Mostly grade 1–2, some grade 3 weirs (all can be portaged).

Introduction

The Earn is a long and possibly under-rated river, winding its way amongst various different types of scenery across the county of Perthshire. It leaves Loch Earn in the west, and at first is a tiny but interesting waterway amongst a wooded valley. At Comrie, a popular tourist village, the Earn widens out, and is nearly always canoeable from here. The trip down to Crieff, a spa town, is the most popular for a day's paddle. After Crieff, the river gains in water, and has various interesting weirs down to Kinkell Bridge. Lower down, the river winds almost interminably amongst agricultural countryside, with a final tidal stretch to join the Tay.

Water Level

Obvious level for paddling can be seen from bridge at Crieff.

Access

The A85 follows the valley down from Loch Earn. Normal start is at:

power station (NN 743 225; 56.3780, -4.0378),

Access and egress at:

Comrie (NN 775 219; 56.3735, -3.9857),

Crieff (NN 857 209; 56.3666, -3.8524),

Kinkell Bridge (NN 932 167; 56.3306, -3.7293),

Dalreoch Bridge (NO 005 179; 56.3430, -3.6116),

Bridge of Earn (NO 132 187; 56.3526, -3.4064).

Final egress can be at:

Newburgh (NO 235 186; 56.3535, -3.2397).

Campsites & accommodation

Lochearnside (south side); Comrie (2 sites); Crieff (2 sites).

Description

Km

0 At the end of Loch Earn there is a high weir and sluice. Access below this. The river is tiny, and flows amongst many trees, with various small, stony weirs. This part requires skill from open canoeists. Can only be paddled in high water. The main A85 road follows the river.

5.5 Dalchonzie Power Station (**normal start**). Parking here (on B-road off A85), with launch over fence onto exit from power station. The water levels are more reliable here as the water abstracted from Loch Earn is returned. The river is small, tree-lined and pretty.

7 Sharp bend to left, fish farm on right, long weir, shootable on left.

7.5 River bends left down a small gorge, with a rapid, and then a weir across left side of river. Passage is extreme right, with sharp bend to left at the bottom. Road on the right bank.

8.5 First bridge on approach to Comrie.

9 Main road bridge in Comrie, town to left. Access/egress on right side of river, upstream of the bridge with parking for 16 or so vehicles. Rapid under bridge, and then a grade 3 weir, which often has to be portaged on the left side. Small rapids continue, with two larger ones nearer Crieff.

14.5 Sharp bend to right in river, just before very visible monument on a hill ahead. River turns right, then left.

15 Road bridge.

18.5 Crieff Bridge – access point about 150m above bridge, on right bank, before the caravan site. There is a path which leads away to the car park for the rugby club, usually empty and offering parking. Town is up the hill to the left side. Down the road to the right at this point is a visitor centre and shopping, useful café open on Sundays, and all through winter.

23 Dornoch Mill, large weir, grade 3. Land on right side, away from house, to inspect and portage. Can usually be shot, but tends to catch trees and rubbish.

23.5 Road bridge.

27 Colquhalzie Weir, marked by an ornamental estate bridge. Steep weir, shootable on extreme left. Has been graded 4 in past, but more likely a grade 3, regularly shot by open canoes. Be very careful in high water, and inspect by landing 100m upstream

27.5 First broken weir at Mills of Earn, grade 3.

28 Second broken weir, again grade 3, and shootable with care down obvious main flow.

28.5 Kinkell Bridge, the only road bridge for miles, and signposted from all over this part of Perthshire. Egress on left bank, with two parking areas, one by the gate to an estate (please do not block entrance), the other a few yards along road downstream where there is a parking area for anglers. The river now slows down, and meanders across its flood plain. A normal trip from here would be to Bridge of Earn, a long day's paddling.

38 Dalreoch Bridge, followed by main A9 road bridge. Access at the former.

43 Steep road bridge, Forteviot village to right. Steep wooded banks. Islands follow, and there are interesting oxbow lakes in this next stretch.

49.5 Railway bridge, with a rapid under it.

51.5 Tidal limit.

52.5 Railway bridge, with a rapid under it.

55 Bridge of Earn road bridge, village right, last egress for some miles.

55.5 M90 motorway bridge. The river is now still narrow, muddy and tidal, with a long sweep to the south.

63 Last possible exits from river, on to private roads on both banks, on to roads down to houses which were ferry points in years gone by.

63.5 Junction with the Tay estuary.

66.5 Newburgh village on right bank, egress and parking.

Tides

If finishing at Bridge of Earn, the state of tide will make little difference. If making a trip further downstream, it would be much more pleasant, due to extensive mud, to arrive at Bridge of Earn at high tide, and take the ebb downstream and arrive before the water is too low.

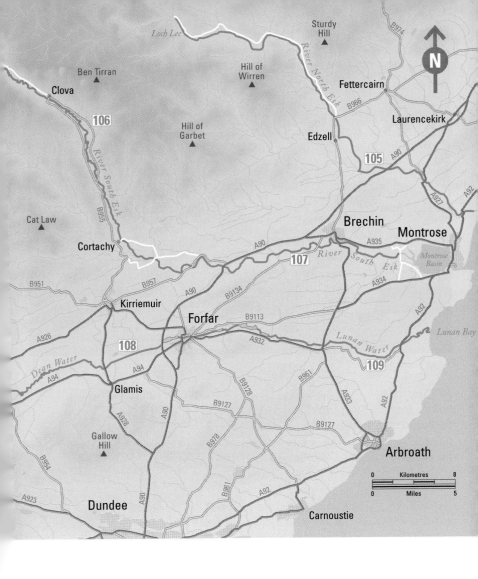

Angus

South Esk near Brechin   📷 *Eddie Palmer*

Angus

Angus is the 'forgotten county', lying between Dundee and Aberdeenshire, but it has beautiful long glens stretching deep into the heart of the Grampian Mountains, and therefore rivers. One result of eastern Scotland enjoying a sunny, dry climate is that the rivers are often low compared with the west, so one has to move quickly when rain falls. The area still has comparatively few tourists, but plenty of things to see, and beaches, camping and caravan sites.

The main geological feature affecting the gradient of rivers is the very obvious 'Highland Line', resulting in great river gorges, where the upland granite, with its peat covering (and midges), gives way to the lower sandstones, broken down into sand and gravels. This actual line, with folded rocks, not an imaginary one, can be easily seen, especially in the Gannochy Gorge of the North Esk.

105 Lower North Esk

Length	13.5km
OS	45
Grade	1

Grade

Grade 1 with 1 weir.

Introduction

This river is one of the long Angus waterways which rise deep in the Grampians, and flow south and east to the North Sea. The North Esk is formed from the Water of Mark and the Water of Lee above Tarfside, in bare and beautiful countryside. This section describes the North Esk from Edzell village to the sea.

Water Level

Judged from the start at Edzell, where there are shallow rapids, the stretch downstream should look paddleable.

Access

Easiest access on to the river is from the main street in Edzell village (NO 602 689), egress at disused railway viaduct near the sea at Montrose (NO 725 622).

Campsites & accommodation

To the north, up the coast, at West Mathers and Johnshaven.

Short easy trip

Northwater Bridge to Marykirk Bridge – 3km.

Description

Km

0   Edzell village. Access is by a track to the river and footbridge from the main street down the side of a garage. It might be easier to unload and walk the 200m or so to the river, as the track is very narrow. Parking on main street. Launch on shallow, sandy stretch, followed by minor rapids. Pleasant wooded banks, occasional ledge rapids.

6   North Water Bridge, main A90 road to Aberdeen. Access and parking at old bridge a few metres downstream.

8.5 Railway bridge, with a rapid under it, water goes down right side. Access from village via a footpath – limited parking in front of houses.

9   Marykirk Bridge – access and parking downstream, right side, on minor road. Usual start point for a half-day trip. Rapid on left-hand bend just below.

10.5 Logie Mill Weir (the old mill has been converted into a house, very visible on right bank). This weir has a central chute visible with retaining walls. Although looking like a minor drop, the central chute has a very powerful stopper. Shoot over left side. In flood, this whole weir disappears.

11.5 Mill of Morphie – the weir was blown up a few years ago. The river now takes a large bend to the right, and then the left, and where the river narrows there are large waves and swirly water. Below here are some shallow small rapids.

13.5 A92 road bridge. The take-out is just below on the left, a walk through to the road to the beach, below the disused railway viaduct – parking space. This road is a very tight turn off the A92 (signposted 'Beach'), beware of traffic. An alternative is to carry on for another kilometre, out on to the sea, and land on the left at the Nature Reserve (NO 745 633) parking.

Other important points

There is also the long 'flat' section of the river between the two difficult white water stretches upstream, but access and egress is difficult, and the level of this very stony stretch is rarely up high enough for a comfortable trip. If in Angus, a much better bet is the South Esk, which carries and holds more water.

South Esk

The South Esk is one of eastern Scotland's best easy touring rivers, and offers one of the longest open canoe trips in the area apart from the Tay. Water and scenery differ down the valley, with the initial flat section in the upper glaciated valley contrasting with the livelier river lower down.

106 Upper South Esk

Length	18km
OS	44
Grade	1

Introduction

Most of this stretch is flat and runs gently through the upper valley, between the mountains of the Grampians, a spectacular valley to paddle. The flatness is due to this being an ancient glaciated valley

Water Level

The upper part can be judged from the bank.

Access

The B955 runs up Glen Clova, and at Gella Bridge (NO 373 653; 56.7750, -3.0277), the egress, the road splits, and both banks are followed by roads up to the Clova Hotel. From here, a single track lane leads up to the access point at the Glen Doll car park (NO 283 761; 56.8707, -3.1780).

Campsites & accommodation

None in the glen. Glen Clova Hotel is main accommodation around. Kirriemuir and Brechin have campsites.

Description

The upper river can be paddled in high water all the way from Glen Doll, at the top, and in most water from the Glen Clova Bridge, down to Gella Bridge (council car park).

Km

0 Glen Doll car park. River is shallow, and often stony.

7 Clova Bridge, hotel, parking and teashop to the left. Good starting point in sum-

mer/lower water levels. The river is still narrow, but it becomes slower below here. It soon meanders between flat banks. In flood, the river overflows its banks.

18 Gella Bridge – suggested egress. Car parks both sides.

Other important points

Downstream of here the river immediately becomes bouldery, and is grade 2/3, with no easy egress for miles. This section (between the Upper and Lower South Esk) is described in *Scottish White Water*.

107 Lower South Esk

Length	38km
OS	54
Grade	1/2
Tides	Montrose Basin dries

Portages

Two possible portages at weirs, one above Brechin (NO 568 587; 56.7180, -2.7074), the other at Kinnairds Mill (NO 626 583; 56.7149, -2.6126) below Brechin.

Tides and weather

The estuary is exposed and potentially hazardous (check wind forecast).

If finishing at the Bridge of Dun there are no tidal effects. If paddling on to Montrose across Montrose Basin, this is best done at slack high water, to avoid running aground on the ebb.

Introduction

From here the South Esk meanders across the plain of Strathmore. The section below Brechin is usually paddleable all year round, and the river debouches into the strange tidal lagoon of Montrose Basin, a spectacular reserve for geese and wading birds.

Water Level

If the upper stretches look shallow, it is worth looking lower down where the river may still be paddleable. The bridge at Brechin is a good place to check the water levels.

Access

Start either at Cortachy Bridge (NO 395 598; 56.7259, -2.9903), or Prosen Bridge (NO 395 587; 56.7160, -2.9901).

Normal final egress from river at Bridge of Dun (NO 663 585; 56.7170, -2.5522), or if carrying on down the estuary Montrose Basin (NO 708 570; 56.7038, -2.4785), or Montrose Sailing Club (NO 706 568; 56.7020, -2.4817).

Campsites & accommodation

Brechin or Forfar.

Description

Km

0 – Cortachy Bridge. This road is narrow, with no parking, so you will need to drop boats off, and go back into the village about 300m to park. This first couple of kilometres can be tricky in winter high water, with tight bends and overhanging trees.

2   Junction with River Prosen. Prosen Bridge, 1.5km up the River Prosen (on main road up glen) is a good start point, if there is enough water (easy water, and parking). Sometimes, the South Esk has plenty of water in it, but the Prosen doesn't, so it can be a frustrating bump and scrape down to the junction. From the junction there are fairly continuous grade 2 rapids,

a good test for open canoes in flood.

3.5   A sharp left-hand bend heralds a rock slab fall, followed by fast water and waves in a mini-gorge down to Shielhill Bridge. Access/egress at old bridge, with some limited parking. Don't block entrance to house. Minor rapids follow.

5   A sharp bend to left, followed by a right bend is the beginning of a short but exciting little gorge at Castle Hill. Ahead is an obvious drop, just a rocky 1m, with a chute on left side of river. After this, two rapids with waves in a closed-in gorge. At end, a narrow gap, with swirly water. A couple more rapids.

6   Inshewan House on left bank. River now slows down for weir.

6.5   Long bend to left. Inshewan Weir has broken down, and has a way down on the extreme right-hand side, around a large rock, and a route down the right side of an island. No great difficulties.

7.5   Justinhaugh Road alongside on left, parking down near bridge, island with fast water and a drop. Good place to judge river height; if the rapid down left side has enough water, the river will be good.

8.5   River is shallow and rocky, approaching Tannadice.

9.5   River bends to right when village appears, broken weir, covered in high water. Some limited parking, and launching, near church in Tannadice.

11.5   Finavon Bridge, main A90 road. Launching here is difficult. (However, no places to access between here and near Brechin. Trips will have to start either at Justinhaugh or Tannadice).

18.5   Noran Water joins from left. Gas pumping station on left bank (possible access here, but it is a private road). Shallows due to farm ford.

21.5 Large weir. Inspect. Shoot on left normally.

23.5 Road bridge, B-road. Egress left bank above bridge.

26 Brechin Castle estate bridge, interesting carvings on bridge.

26.5 Landing on left at Brechin car park – concrete landings, good place to start or finish trips. Rapid just downstream.

27 Road bridge – rocky slabs under it.

28.5 Old weir across, left bend on to cliff, right bend down rapid. Good stopping place.

29.5 Kinnairds Mill Weir. Large weir, usual route down right side, just to right of fish steps. Rocky at bottom. Followed by drops which are artificial to aid salmon upstream. Popular angling spot.

32.5 Disused railway bridge, rapids.

33.5 Bridge of Dun road bridge, end of most trips. Egress on right across field, parking on bridge approaches. River becomes tidal.

34.5 The Lurgies, mudflats on both sides, many wading birds to left.

35 Old Montrose, ancient port, on right bank. Egress and some parking, useful stopping point. Head from here directly across to sailing club, to right of obvious channel under bridge.

38 Montrose Sailing Club, egress on to ramp, and parking to side of club.

108 Dean Water

Length	17km
OS	53/54
Grade	1

Introduction

The Dean Water is the ditch which drains Forfar Loch to the west (it really is a ditch, a drain dug by the Glamis Estate in the 1850s, when the 'main' river, the Kerbet Burn, was straightened below Douglastown). The trip is probably only of local interest. The river is flat, except for two minor weirs, and a fast stretch just before the junction with the Isla.

Water Level

The first few kilometres will be very shallow in summer, best when in near flood.

Note: Currently (2018), the river is impracticable from Forfar due to a great number of fallen trees. The only practical start is at Cookston Farm Bridge (NO 340 480; 56.6192, -3.0772) at 10km.

Access

Access at the start from Forfar, Lochmill Farm (NO 429 498; 56.6365, -2.9326), and the A94 follows the river some distance from its left bank, access via small lanes.

Egress at Crathies Bridge on the River Isla (NO 279 454; 56.5949, -3.1759).

Campsites & accommodation

At Roundyhill, between Glamis and Kirriemuir.

Description

Km

0 The outflow from Loch of Forfar. Because of difficulties created by the A90 road culvert, access is much easier from a minor road at Lochmill Farm, half a kilometre dowstream.

0.5 Lochmill Farm Bridge (access). The river is totally straight for 4km.

4 River winds through the Glamis Estate, with lovely trees, and ornamental bridges.

5.5 Road bridge, Glamis to Kirriemuir road. River now starts to wind.

10 Small gauging weir, just before Cookston Farm Bridge on a minor road. The river now has high banks, a bit boring in low water.

11.5 River winds around a farm.

15.5 Very tight double bend, river becomes more wooded. River is joined by the Meigle Burn, from left. The current picks up, especially in high water. Broadleaved woodland on left.

16 Large weir, shootable on left side, and landing to inspect on grass on left side. Converted mill on left bank follows, please do not land. Road bridge.

17 Junction with River Isla, and egress at Crathies Bridge, right side.

Other important points

The Dean Water has in the past been used to reach the sea from Forfar, the county town of Angus, via the Isla, Tay, and the sea to Arbroath, 14 miles from Forfar. The Kerbet can also be paddled in high water from some distance to the east, to make an even longer trip.

109 Lunan Water

Length	9km
OS	54
Grade	1
Tides	No tidal effect

Portages

Could be portages required due to fallen trees, and rubble.

Introduction

This is a mad, high water paddle, not known to many kayakers, and only possible when other rivers are at death height. For most of the way, an open canoe could not be turned, and there are few breakouts. The Lunan is Forfar's second river, leaving via the lochs on the east side of town.

Access

From the B965, access at Boysack Mills (NO 623 491; 56.6322, -2.6162), egress at Lunan (NO 690 511; 56.6507, -2.5072).

Campsites & accommodation

Carnoustie and Monifieth.

Description

Boysack Mills is the usual start point, and there is a constant good flow in high water, with small rapids and broken, rubbly weirs. It is about 9km down to Lunan Bay and the sea, with some surprises on the way. At The Grange, thick rhododendron almost bars the way; a knife or saw is handy. At the tidal limit, below the A92 road bridge, and the mainline railway bridge, floating bushes and rubbish often block the way, a veritable floating mat with no discernible exit. There is thick undergrowth from there down to Lunan village, a double bend, sight of a ruined castle, and the final sudden bend round to the beach. A quick exit is advised due to the surf. Exit to the beach car park is either to the left over sand dunes, or along the beach for 200m, and over the back of the beach.

Otther important points

At Friockheim, 12km east of Forfar, two burns join, and there has been paddling from the confluence – with low bridges, and barbed wire!

Fife

Rafting up on Loch Leven　　　　　　　　　　　　　　　📷 *Eddie Palmer*

Fife

Fife is a low-lying eastern county with mixed farming and woodland, and has pretty villages in its northern half. The Lomond Hills then split the area, overlooking on their western flanks the large Loch Leven, and Kinross, well worth a visit for its bird wildlife and the circular foot and cycle path around it.

To the south is the former coal mining area, with many small towns and villages, and an obvious industrial past.

The River Eden flows east through the northern half, and is pleasant, and has remnants of a past textile industry, with mills on the river.

The River Leven leaves Loch Leven, and flows east to the sea at Methil and Leven, still ports and a former shipbuilding centre. The Leven valley is due for a major clean-up, and the river is set to improve from former polluted existence.

110 River Eden

Length	20km
OS	59
Grade	1

Portages

Possible portages due to trees down across the river.

Introduction

The Eden is a small local river, probably not one to travel a great distance to, but still with some charm.

It rises just west of the M90 in the south of Perthshire, and flows east, around the north of the Lomond Hills, to the sea at Guardbridge near St Andrews.

Water Level

Inspect the river at Cupar, and just below it – the minimum canoeable level is fairly obvious.

Access

Access can be had via a bridge on the B9129 just north of Kingskettle (NO 309 089), but a start at Cupar is strongly advised as, especially in the summer, trees and vegetation block the river, and there are some awkward weirs. The egress is just below the old bridge at Guardbridge (NO 452 189; 56.3592, -2.8885).

Campsites & accommodation

Ladybank and St Andrews.

Description

This is a tiny burn until just after the A914 Dundee to Glenrothes main road, where several small ditches swell it. The Eden is mainly an irrigation ditch for the fertile arable land of the Howe of Fife. The best bet is the 5km down to Dairsie Mains Bridge from Cupar (launch in park at Cupar, egress right side, downstream of Dairsie Bridge, onto road). This stretch is in a wooded valley, with old mills, broken weirs, and often fallen trees. It is then a further 2km to the tidal limit, and 3.5km to Guardbridge. The estuary is amongst farmland, with a large caravan site on the left bank. The estuary is a Fife Council Nature Reserve, and a permit is required for this stretch.

Exit at Guardbridge on right bank onto a footpath, and then under new road bridge to old bridge a few metres downstream.

111 Loch Leven

OS 58

Introduction

Loch Leven is a major National Nature Reserve, managed by NatureScot, which provides precious over-wintering habitat for migratory birds. Because of this access is delicate and only allowed in the summer months.

Access

The loch is easily reached from the central belt of Scotland via the M90 north from the Forth bridges.

Access permitted at:

Kinross Pier, west side of loch (NO 122 017; 56.1998, -3.4169) – trips advised to commence from here,

Kirkgate Park (west side, NO 128 017; 56.1999, -3.4073),

Burleigh Sands (north side, on the Lethangie road from Kinross, NO 133 040; 56.2206, -3.3999),

Findatie (east side, NT 170 992; 56.1782, -3.3388).

You are not allowed to land in any other place than those mentioned above. This prohibition includes any of the islands. The large St Serf's island in the south-east corner is especially vulnerable.

Description

If in the area, go to the NatureScot ranger office on the loch side at Kinross, and ask for advice. Currently (2020), there is a dog-leg paddle advised, between the main landing near Kinross, on the west side, and Burleigh Sands on the north side.

A trip is possible from Kinross around Castle Island (owned by Historic Environment Scotland), north to Burleigh Sands, and back again. This is worth doing, and can show you many birds and their habitats.

Other important points

On the south side of the loch is an RSPB Reserve well worth visiting, and there is now a very well-used foot and cycle path around the whole loch, also worth spending a day here. Refreshment places at Kinross, Findatie, (NT 170 993; 56.1791, -3.3388) and on the east side, reached from Kinnesswood.

112 River Leven

Length	24km
OS	59
Grade	1 and weirs

Introduction

This river is worthy of inclusion because there is a major Leven Corridor Development Plan to clean up and revitalise the whole corridor. Most major mammal and bird species are present in the lower valley.

This small watercourse runs east from Loch Leven to the Firth of Forth at the town of Leven. Between Methil and Leven it is industrial and polluted. Trees, weirs, sluices and rubbish obstruct much of the way, and it is not attractive. The middle section through Glenrothes is impassable, due to the watercourse being culverted through a very large paper mill.

Access

Upper section – The get-on at the exit from Loch Leven is at a parking place on the B9097 at the south-east corner of the loch (NT 170 993; 56.1791, -3.3388). Egress at Cabbagehall Bridge (NO 248 010; 56.1957, -3.2136).

Lower Section – Access south east of Markinch off the A911 (NO 298 010; 56.1964, -3.1330). Egress at the Forth of Firth on the left bank (NO 382 005; 56.1931, -2.9975).

Description

Km

0   Start from where the river leaves Loch Leven (NO 170 993; 57.0772, -3.3710). The Leven starts as totally flat canal paddle (the river is canalised in several

stretches), and then a small river with many trees, and several weirs near Leslie, some of which will require portages.

7   Egress at Cabbagehall Bridge at Leslie. There is then a shuttle of some 7km required to by-pass mills at both Leslie and Glenrothes (the latter site is now being developed, and should become more accessible in time). The lower section is 12km of mainly narrow river, with many weirs, and no easy access off roads. It is an old industrial area, with almost no views of the river, and no easy access off bridges.

14   The best chance of getting on the river is at the south-eastern corner of Markinch, where the railway and a main road are high above the river valley, and the A911 road runs close to the river (NO 298 010; 56.1964, -3.1330), now a natural river, usually with good water in it.

16   Balgonie Castle is passed, and then Milton of Balgonie. More weirs follow and the river enters a gap between Windygates and Methil, with much old industrial landscape.

21   A nasty pipe passes overhead, with spikes on, just before a large weir (NO 335 700; 56.8167, -3.0911).

24   At Sawmill Bridge the river becomes tidal (NO 375 006; 56.1939, -3.0088). It then gradually widens, and passes between the towns of Leven and Methil.

24   The river enters the Firth of Forth – plenty of parking near swimming pool on the left bank, or via the seashore.

Forth and Clyde Canal ☐ Tracy Macpherson

Central

Contents

Central

Racing on the Forth and Clyde Canal   *Fraser Gormal*

First canoe trip with Zac 📷 *Seb Smith*

River Teith, Callendar   📷 *Eddie Palmer*

Central

This central section of Scotland comprises many urban areas, and the eastern part of the Loch Lomond and Trossachs National Park area, which is well worthwhile visiting. A base around either Callander or Aberfoyle in the Trossachs offers the paddler plenty of scope, and a different experience to the Loch Lomond area.

113 Balquhidder to Loch Lubnaig

Balquhidder, River Larig, Loch Doine, Loch Voil , River Balvaig, Loch Lubnaig

Length	21.5km
OS	57
Grade	1

Introduction

This is an ideal beginner's trip. There are no difficulties on the water, no awkward portages, there is a campsite halfway down, the trip is river and loch, and the scenery is great! The best plan is to allow two days for this; one day would be rushing too much. This area is also within easy reach of Stirling and the rest of the Central Belt.

Water Level

The driest part of the Balvaig is under the bridge at the end of Loch Voil, near Balquhidder village. The level can easily be estimated from here.

Access

There is only one drawback to the trip, and that is the parking of vehicles. In the whole of the glen, the road is narrow and awkward, and in order to prevent problems particular parking is referred to. It is also strongly recommended to do this trip in either spring or autumn, and avoid school holidays (Scottish and English) so as to reduce parking congestion. Many tourists come to see Rob Roy's grave in Balquhidder graveyard. If you do go there in summer, grab parking places early in the morning!

The start is on River Larig, from a passing-place (no parking, NN 453 186; 56.3344, -4.5052).

Access/egress points:

At the eastern end of Loch Voil, at a lay-by near the bridge over the River Balvaig (NN 535 207; 56.3559, -4.3737).

At Strathyre campsite (NN 558 163; 56.3171, -4.3340).

At the top end of Loch Lubnaig (NN 564 151; 56.3065, -4.3237), the first large car park on Loch Lubnaig (NN 586 118; 56.2775, -4.2863), and the last car park (NN 585 107; 56.2676, -4.2874).

Do not park in passing places on Loch Voil! Local people, especially farmers, will soon move you on.

Short easy trip

Loch Lubnaig, from parking on the main A83 road – 6km round trip.

Campsites & accommodation

At Strathyre.

Description

The start can be on the River Larig, right up at the west end of the glen, near the road end. The road comes close to the river about 500m before the car park at the end. Boats have to be off-loaded quickly to avoid congestion. The river is slow and just wide enough for open canoes. After 1.5km, it flows into Loch Doine (no road access), and after another 1.5km, a tiny river of 200m or so connects this top loch with the 6km long Loch Voil. (Where the tiny river joins Loch Voil, there is a summerhouse where Buddhists come to contemplate.) The south side of Loch Voil is much more peaceful being away from the road.

As you approach Balquhidder village, the River Balvaig leaves the loch on the right-hand side, and soon flows, fairly swiftly, under a stone road bridge. Access is good here, with parking to the left side of bridge. The river soon becomes tortuous in its bends, but there are little rapids for the first kilometre or so. The river then slows down, and takes about 6.5km to reach Strathyre village on the A84 from Callander to Crianlarich. Halfway down this stretch the minor road on the right side of river comes close, and there is a tiny cable ferry for animals to cross the river.

The village of Strathyre has most facilities, the campsite being just 200m downstream of the stone bridge (restricted parking). Approaching the bridge, there is a small drop, either an old ford or weir, and two rapids after the bridge.

From the campsite down to Loch Lubnaig is a good kilometre, and it is possible for a strong paddler to paddle back up.

Loch Lubnaig is a gem. It lies among high mountains, is 6km long and half a km wide, and is used for Scottish sprint canoe racing and open canoe sailing. Just as the river flows into the loch, there is a parking place on the left, on the main road nearby, one of only three on the loch. The next two, which are off the road, and with picnic facilities, are a further 4.5 and 5.5km down respectively.

Other important points

There are two other approaches to the trip. One is to get on somewhere along Loch Voil, but there is little parking (it would need a drop-off in a passing place), or to park at the bottom of Loch Voil, and paddle up. Either could give access up the connector to Loch Doine, so they shouldn't be excluded from plans.

At the southern end of Loch Lubnaig, the River Leny, grade 3/4 (5) (see *Scottish White Water*) leaves Loch Lubnaig, and you probably don't want to go here!

114 Loch Achray, Loch Venachar and River Teith

Length	36.5km
OS	57
Grade	1/2(3-)

Grades

Grade 1 and 2, Eas Gobhain 2/3 below bridge, Torrie Rapid (3) in high water, Deanston Weir is dangerous.

Portages

See text for portages on Eas Gobhain and Deanston Weir.

Introduction

This trip is often shortened, due to low water levels in the rivers above Callander, and results in a paddle on the River Teith from somewhere around Callander. The Teith has a deserved popularity as a beginner's white-water river. The Teith is a pretty river, and an annual trip for many open boaters. The river has the quality of never being boring, having continuous small rapids, but there is only one place likely to get anything like dangerous in flood (Deanston Weir). The river is then grade 1 with a couple of weirs down to the junction with the Forth.

Water Level

The upper connecting rivers have to be inspected to see if the upper section of the trip is feasible.

If the Teith can be launched onto comfortably from the car park in Callander, in other words just below the walkway, the river is a nice level.

Access

Top of Loch Achray (NN 509 070; 56.2321, -4.4080), Loch Venachar off the A821 (NN 56 06; 56.2247, -4.3252), riverside car park in Callander (NN 625 069; 56.2347, -4.2208), lay-by on A84 near Torrie Rapid (NN 670 046; 56.2153, -4.1470), below Deanston Weir (NN 714 016; 56.1896, -4.0746), final egress in Stirling on the Forth (NN 796 951; 57.0312, -3.9860).

Campsites & accommodation

Callander and Cornton (Stirling).

Short easy trips

Loch Achray – 2km; Loch Venacher – 6km round trip.

Description

Km

0   Western end of Loch Achray – car park near loch. Picturesque surroundings of the Trossach mountains.

2   Loch ends in the Black Water – usually enough water, a small river.

2.5 Burn enters on the left from the Glen Finglas reservoir.

5   River enters Loch Venachar.

7   Main road alongside on north shore – car park.

8   Loch Venachar Sailing Club on south shore, reached by a narrow road from the east only.

10   The Eas Gobhain leaves the loch, over two weirs, waterworks on right bank. This river is more often than not very dry, and should be inspected before paddling.

10.5 Weir.

11   Road bridge (minor road from A821 to south side Loch Vennacher). If the section

downstream has not been inspected, land immediately after the bridge on the left side on a shingle beach (portaging over the bridge is difficult due to high stone walls). The river falls over rocky ledges, between islands and trees, for the next 300m. There is a fall of some 2m near the end of this stretch. The whole section can be portaged down the left-hand bank in a field. In low water, open canoeists can wade and line boats down. Kayakers will find the section straightforward in medium water. In high water it is a serious proposition. Access back to the river is when buildings downstream become visible, and the river bends to the right to come nearer to the minor road down to Callander.

Torrie Rapid, River Teith 　　📷 *Eddie Palmer*

13   River Leny joins from left. You are virtually in Callander town now. Car park and recreation area on left bank (Meadows Car Park) Usual launch point.

13.5 Road bridge.

16.5 Road on right bank. Valley becomes narrower and pretty, much broadleaved woodland.

17.5 Keltie Water joins left, several bends.

19   Sharp bend to left. Torrie Rapid (NN 663 043; 56.2124, -4.1581) is a ledge run on extreme left, with a turn to right in low water to avoid undercut rock. In high water, large wave train. Two more small drops in next 400m.

19.5 Main A82 road on left bank. Lay-by and egress (marked by water gauge and obvious path away from river).

21.5 Private estate bridge, ornate metalwork.

23   Noticeable rock ledge.

24   Deanston Weir. This weir is high, long, and dangerous. In low water, landing could be made on left side of it to carry over, as the face of weir will be dry. In high water, portage on the left by landing about 100m above the weir, on to a track high on the left bank, and get back in down stone steps below the weir. An alternative could be lining down the fish steps on the right bank, but landing at the sluices is difficult. Shooting the steps on the right side in kayaks is possible, but not recommended. The face of the weir has a 1m drop at the end, and there is a substantial stopper in high water. Egress to Deanston from here is difficult (fence with barbed wire).

24.5 There is a take out right side just after sewage works, up over wire gabions, to Deanston village. There is good parking space here by the gates of the sewage works.

25   A84 road bridge.

26.5 Weir. River now widens, slows down – several islands.

32   River Forth joins on the right. The Teith often carries more water than the Forth.

33   M9 road bridge. Just below, a shallow weir (covered at some high tides). Upper tidal limit. Rapids below at some states of tide.

34   Allan Water joins left.

35.5 Egress on left bank.

36.5 Stirling Bridge (old bridge, followed by modern road bridge). Egress recommended to left of old bridge, now pedestrianised. Below here the river has very muddy banks.

115 Loch Ard and River Forth

Length	Up to 56km
OS	57
Grade	1

Introduction

The loch, crannog and river as far as Aberfoyle are well worth exploring. Unfortunately this is not the case with the rest of the river. The Forth sounds like a major river, with a giant estuary, but is a disappointment. It's usually easy to say something good about Scottish rivers, but most of the Forth is ... boring. It is a very long, narrow, winding river for most of its length, with very restricted views due to high banks. Many paddlers do it to say they've done it, and then wonder why!

Water Level

The level of the river running through Aberfoyle is a good indicator of the higher stretch - a scrape, and it will be a pain, although most of the Forth downstream will be alright, as it is like a canal.

Access

Loch Ard (NN 45 02; 56.1853, -4.5003), north side off B829, Aberfoyle Bridge (NN 520 010; 56.1786, -4.3869), Shannochill campsite south of Aberfoyle (NS 532 989; 56.1601, -4.3664), Dykehead Bridge on B8034 (NS 599 973;

56.1478, -4.2577), B822 bridge (NS 668 960; 56.1381, -4.1459), Gargunnock Bridge B8075 (NS 715 952; 56.1322, -4.0698).

Egress either at Craigforth at the old bridge before Stirling (NS 770 956; 56.1372, -3.9815), or in Stirling.

Campsites & accommodation

Shannochill, Thornhill, or Stirling.

Short easy trip

Loch Ard – 6km round trip.

Description

The start up at Loch Ard is pretty and the paddle to Aberfoyle rewarding, with wooded banks.

If you insist on going further, wild camping is quite possible, but not very attractive. Escape to the Stirlingshire villages to the south brings some nice pubs, if you're stuck. The flatness of the landscape is due to the river passing through Flanders Moss, one of the last raised bogs in central Scotland. Canoe campers have been known to have fled screaming after a couple of days of this paddling, especially if they are joined by midges in the summer.

Km

0   Kinlochard village on Loch Ard. Parking and landing/access. The loch is some 3km long, with wooded banks, a crannog and a castle, well worth exploring.

3   Exit to the Forth is in the south-east corner, quite narrow and hidden.

4   The loch/river narrows at Milton village, to left. Duchray Water joins right (see *w*).

5.5 Aberfoyle Bridge, village left. All services and shops.

8.5 A wooded stretch at the A81

Canoe camping, Loch Ard   📷 *Seb Smith*

(Glasgow road) bridge. The nice scenery now ends, and the river enters a dark green mass of plantations soon after this. Gartrenich Moss to left, Flanders Moss to the right.

12.5 Kelty Water joins right.

21 Road bridge. Port of Menteith 4km left, Arnprior 2.5km to the right.

24.5 Farm bridge.

31 B822 road bridge. Kippen 2km to right. The river winds even more now.

42 B8075 road bridge.

56 A84 road bridge near Craigforth.

Below here the River Teith joins from left, often with more flow and it is a further 4.5km down to Stirling Bridge.

116 River Devon
(Clackmannanshire)

Length	19km
OS	58
Grade	1

Portages

Possible portage before Dollarfield.

Introduction

The Devon is a delightful and pretty river. The section described is where it is in its easier lowland stages.

Water Level

Looking downstream from the start point at Vicar's Bridge, the little shallow rapids should be able to float a canoe.

Access

Vicar's Bridge, on minor roads between the A91 and A977 (NS 986 980; 56.1638, -3.6347), Dollarfield Bridge (near Dollar, NS 961 970; 56.1543, -3.6746), Glenfoot Bridge, (below Tillicoultry, NS 910 964; 56.1478, -3.7565), Alva bridge (NS 884 962; 56.1454, -3.7983). Egress at A907 bridge, west of Tullibody (NS 846 952; 56.1355, -3.8590).

Campsites & accommodation

At Dollarfield Bridge.

Description

Km

0   Vicar's Bridge. Good parking here. The bridge is reached by a very small, single-track and wooded lane from either the A91 to the north, or the A 977 to the south. If looking downriver, there are obvious shallows, the river will be a pain down to Dollar. River pretty, very wooded, with trees across in places. In high summer, the banks are covered with the pink of Himalayan balsam and the white of wild garlic.

2.5   Small weir – can be easily carried round on right side, campsite.

3.0   Dollarfield Bridge, and camp and caravan site on north (left) bank. The owners are welcoming to those wishing to park cars. The first 2km or so of river from here are very winding and wooded, with frequent possible obstructions (not the straight river shown on OS maps).

5.0   Footbridge – slightly deeper water from now on.

5.5   First of four sheep fences – this one has to be carried over.

6.0   Footbridge, followed by shingle bank on

right bank, and egress to main road at lay-by. River becomes much more sandy and shingle. Area on left bank of old oxbow lakes. Second sheep fence.

7.0   Main road near again on right bank. Many sharp bends.

7.5   Old rail bridge, now a footbridge. Tillicoultry is now near on right bank, but there is little sign of it. The first sign is a furniture store car park on right.

8.5   Tillicoultry road bridge – poor access, better to paddle on to Glenfoot Bridge. River is still rural in appearance, although there are signs of its industrial past .

9.5   Glenfoot Bridge, egress right bank, upstream, car parking on waste land just over minor road.

12.5 Road bridge. Alva to right, Fishcross left.

13.5 Alva road bridge. Narrow road, some parking on waste ground to right.

17.5 Menstrie road bridge, no parking.

18   Old rail bridge.

19   A907 road bridge. Last chance to leave river (2km before it joins a very muddy River Forth). Access/egress on old bridge, possible parking on old road.

Other important points

The Devon rises west of the Upper and Lower Glendevon reservoirs in a remote part of the Ochil Hills, flows east then south, and is first seen by most people as it flows under the A91. Don't be misled, however, as although in high water the river could be paddled from here, the Devon becomes smaller, drier and much overgrown near Crook of Devon, (3km down). The valley then turns west, and just before the A823 at Rumbling Bridge (a clue here), it plunges into a deep gorge. Looking at the countryside, this is quite unexpected, and the

River Devon   📷 *Forth Rivers Trust*

river is some 30 to 40m down. Exploration of the valley below here is very difficult, and the map marks a waterfall a further 2km downriver. When Vicar's Bridge is reached, the next road bridge, life becomes easier, and the Devon is in its final lowland stages. The section described starts here.

117 River Avon
(West Lothian)

Length	15km or 10km in low water
OS	65
Grade	1/2 2/3

Grades
Grade 1 and 2 (top 5km) and grade 2 and 3 (lower 10km).

Introduction
The Avon is a short rural delight, despite being close to industry. It rises in the hills to the south of Falkirk, and the 5km down from Avonbridge

can be paddled when high (at which water levels the lower half is considerably more difficult). The next 6km is the best part, running through a wooded gorge. From Linlithgow down is a rather industrialised 4km, with egress just before the river becomes tidal approaching the oil and chemical complex of Grangemouth.

Water Level
A look over at Avon Gorge will soon tell you if there is enough water in the small rapids, or a look over the high banks within Muiravonside Country Park.

Access
At Avonbridge on the B8028 at the top (NS 911 728; 55.9359, -3.7453), Avon Gorge A801 road bridge park with care – dangerous road, (NS 955 736; 55.9440, -3.6751), Linlithgow (NS 983 773; 55.9779, -3.6317), and final egress at Polmonthill (NS 949 796; 55.9978, -3.6871).

River Avon   📷 *Jonathan Riddell*

Campsites & accommodation

Linlithgow.

Description

Km

0   There is little road access to the higher part and trees across this section could make passage quite difficult, so beware. The river can be seen at Strath House, halfway down, but the country lanes are narrow and there is no parking. Grade 1/2.

5   A801 Avon Gorge road bridge. The lower 6km from here down to Linlithgow is either a rocky grade 2 in medium water, or grade 2/3, with some interesting and testing rapids in a wooded gorge. Most of this passes through Muiravonside Country Park (Falkirk Council), a delightful valley with active badger setts. If in doubt, go in and talk to the Rangers, and you can prospect much of it.

8.5   The river passes under the canal aqueduct for the Union Canal.

11   Linlithgow Bridge, which has a pub on it. If you are getting out here, take out just after the road bridge and weir coming into Linlithgow. Park carefully, not right on the bridge, which is restricted.

12   M9 road bridge.
Rather industrial from here down.

15   Polmonthill – on a minor road bridge, just before the A 905 road bridge, and the river becoming tidal. The paddler is almost within the Grangemouth chemical works.

Glasgow to Edinburgh Canoe Trail

There is a free leaflet available online– *A Complete Guide to Paddling across Central Scotland* – published by Scottish Canals.

Scottish Canals (www.scottishcanals.com) maintain the Forth and Clyde Canal and the Union Canal, which join up at Falkirk, at the Falkirk Wheel, and offer guidance and advice to paddling them. There is also safety advice within the leaflet, especially about the canal tunnels, bridges, locks, and operational requirements.

The leaflet has a Trail Overview, and five Section Maps to aid the paddler. Paddling west to east is advised, as the prevailing wind is westerly.

Highlights

• The route commences at the Pinkston WW centre almost in the middle of Glasgow, now a major location for watersports.

• The eastern part of the Forth and Clyde Canal runs in the valley of the River Kelvin alongside the remains of the Roman Antonine wall to the south.

• The Falkirk Wheel, truly one of the engineering wonders of the modern world, was constructed to lower boats 35m down to the Forth and Clyde, which replaces 11 locks, the largest rotating boat lift in the world. For full details, see www.thefalkirkwheel.co.uk.

- At the far eastern end of the Forth and Clyde Canal, as it passes both the Falkirk Wheel and Falkirk town is the Helix Project, containing the Kelpies statue.
- The Union Canal is a contour waterway, following the line of the land, so no locks after the start at Falkirk Wheel. It passes over the River Avon in West Lothian, on a spectacular aqueduct.

Forth and Clyde Canal   Tracy Macpherson

118 Forth and Clyde Canal

Pinkston Basin (Glasgow), to the Falkirk Wheel

Length	33km
OS	64/65

Introduction

This pleasant trip takes the paddler east out of Glasgow on a route which can be easily completed in a day. The Pinkston centre is worth seeing for its short but impressive artificial white-water course, and arriving at the Falkirk Wheel is another tourism experience. Both offer parking and facilities for the traveller. Considering that Glasgow is the largest urban centre in Scotland, one is soon out in green countryside.

Portages

There are just four locks on this stretch of the canal.

Access

West to east: Pinkston centre, Port Dundas, Glasgow, (NS 595 668; 55.8738, -4.2481); A 879 bridge (NS 583 695; 55.8977, -4.2687); Glasgow Bridge (parking place), west of Kirkintilloch on the A803 (NS 634 730; 55.9306, -4.1889); Road bridge in centre of Kirkintilloch (NS 658 739; 55.9394, -4.1509); Auchinstarry Bridge (NS 720 769; 55.9680, -4.0530); Banknock Bridge (NS 776 788; 55.9865, -3.9642); B 816 bridge, Bonnybridge (NS 824 801; 55.9994, -3.8878); the Falkirk Wheel basin (NS 853 801; 56.0001, -3.8413); there are other possible access points, but relatively few with vehicle access.

Campsites & accommodation

None on the canal (see the Cross-Scotland route for advice on wild camping sites); nearest sites at Strathclyde Park, south of Glasgow, or on Loch Lomond.

Description

This canal winds its way out of a very busy and congested industrial area, heading west, then north, and north-east out of the City. At a T-junction, take the right, as the left-hand branch heads west through urban Glasgow. New housing estates give way to more open land to the left, with far-off hills in the distance, and Bishopbriggs to the right. The scenery becomes more rural, and the River Kelvin on the left side heads to the Clyde.

The small towns of Kirkintilloch and Kilsyth are passed, and then a scenic part as the ridge of the Antonine wall is on the right bank. Busy Cumbernauld is just beyond this, and the canal goes under the M80 motorway. All of the land around the canal was a coal mining area, and now industrial Bonnybridge continues this story.

The quite fantastic Falkirk Wheel can be glimpsed through trees, and suddenly the paddler is in what is usually a hive of activity and tourists. There is vehicle parking on the left side, and canal staff can help with onward journeys up the slope to the top of the Wheel, and the Union Canal.

Short easy trips

Auchinstarry to Banknock – 7km one way, or 14km return.

Other important points

The Forth and Clyde has not finished at the Falkirk Wheel, as it proceeds through many locks in Falkirk to the River Carron and the River Forth. This is worth a visit, and can be easily walked. Falkirk has been 'cleaned up' and much revitalised with the impact of the Falkirk Wheel, and there are now canal-side pubs and gardens where once there was industry.

The Glasgow west to Bowling stretch on the Clyde has been excluded as it has many locks.

119 Union Canal
Falkirk Wheel to Ratho (Edinburgh)

Length	50km
OS	65/66

Introduction

The Union Canal runs for 50km from Falkirk to the west side of Edinburgh, following the contours of the West Lothian countryside, with spectacular aqueducts at the river valleys of the Almond and Avon, and at the Edinburgh by-pass.

Portages

Two locks at the start.

Access

At the Falkirk Wheel (NS 853 801; 56.0001, -3.8413); Linlithgow (NT 006 770; 55.9757, -3.5947); Philipstoun, path by the bridge (NT 048 771; 55.9774, -3.5274); Fawnspark on the B8046, near the M9 (NT 060 768; 55.9750, -3.5081); Winchburgh (NT 088 750; 55.9593, -3.4626); Broxburn (NT 077 721; 55.9331, -3.4792); and Ratho village (NT 139 708; 55.9225, -3.3796).

The canal finishes in the west of Edinburgh, the actual end being at Lochrin Basin (NT 245 728; 55.9423, -3.2105), often a shortage of vehicle parking here. In winter, the full trip described might not be viable due to a couple of low swing bridges not being operated, and so a suitable finish might be a kilometre further west in Merchiston at a road bridge (NT 235 718; 55.9332, -3.2262), near the Forth Canoe Club clubhouse.

Campsites & accommodation

No formal sites anywhere near the canal, as this is a mainly former industrial area. Sites back in Edinburgh, and at Cuthill, near West Calder.

Paddling with Poppy on the Union Canal, Edinburgh   ⓒ *Jonathan Riddell*

Description

At the top of the Falkirk Wheel, the canal is rather stark and bare, as it passes the back reaches of Falkirk, with two locks to raise it on to its original contour.

Soon after this is the Falkirk canal tunnel, of a kilometre in length; Scottish Canals protocols must be followed for this part of the trip.

The suburbs of Redding and Polmont take the canal on to the most scenic part of the journey, through pretty West Lothian countryside. The River Avon runs in a steep-sided wooded valley, and the canal crosses at some height, with little protection on the sides. It then touches Linlithgow, a former important loading port for trading narrow boats. The small mining towns of Philipstoun, Winchburgh, and Broxburn follow, each having wharves which once was used for coal loading. The large red shale 'bings' (spoil heaps) of former oil shale

mining are very obvious in this area.

The Union then dives under the M9 for a final open countryside stretch, with another aqueduct over the River Almond. The canal crosses over the Edinburgh by-pass, and threads through the suburbs of Sighthill, Wester Hales, and Slateford, to a final green stretch into the heart of Edinburgh at its west end.

Short easy trips

Polmont Station (NS 930 780; 55.9830, -3.7169) to Linlithgow, (NT 006 770; 55.9757, -3.5947) over the Avon Aqueduct – 8km one way, 16km return.

Ratho village (NT 139 708; 55.9225, -3.3796), either west to the Lins Mill Aqueduct (NT 105 706; 55.9201, -3.4439) – 3.5km one-way, 7km return, or east to the aqueduct over the A 720, Edinburgh by-pass (NT 183 705; 55.9206, -3.3091) –10km return).

South

Contents

Ayrshire
120 River Ayr 171
121 Loch Doon............................172
122 River Doon 172
123 Water of Girvan 173

The Clyde Valley
124 Upper River Clyde.....................175
125 Lower River Clyde.....................177

Dumfries and Galloway
126 Luce Bay 180
127 Isle of Whithorn and Garlieston..........180
128 Gatehouse of Fleet....................180
129 Brighouse Bay, Kirkcudbright Bay 181
130 Rivers Ken, Dee and Loch Ken...........181
131 Auchencairn Bay, Orchardton Bay
     and Rough Firth......................183
132 Lower Nith and Nith Estuary.............183
133 River Annan 184

Borders
134 River Tweed..........................187
135 River Teviot..........................190

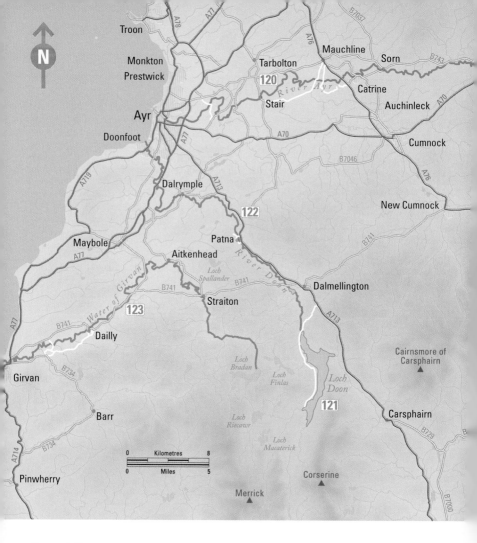

Ayrshire

Ayrshire

The two Ayrshire rivers below both appear in *Scottish White Water*, as easier rivers than the norm in the guide. A brief account of distances is given below to aid paddlers, but both require rain to make them a reasonable prospect to paddle, and therefore worth travelling any distance for.

120 River Ayr

Length	41.5km
OS	70/71
Grade	1/2/3(3)(4)

Sandstone gorge, River Ayr   📷 *Mike Hayward*

Portages

Portages can be made at the weir at Catrine (grade 4), and Auchincruive (grade 3).

Introduction

The Ayr is a long river, rising on the Lanarkshire/Ayrshire border, and flowing west for some 50km to the sea at Ayr. It is a good river for paddlers to become used to easy rapids (the bedrock is 'soft' sandstone), and the hazards can be portaged. The countryside is bare higher up, becoming wooded and attractive in the lower reaches. Grade 1/2, apart from hazards mentioned below. Many of the road bridges are high above the river valley, so inspect for access and egress points.

Note: It is suggested that due to dangerous weirs on the approach to Ayr that trips are ended at Auchencruive.

Water Level

Look over any of the bridges at sandstone shallows. The paddling level is obvious. In high water, the upper river sandstone gorges become dangerous, with continuous high waves. The river calms down after the junction with Lugar Water.

Access

Sorn Bridge (NS 555 265; 55.5108, -4.2908), Catrine bridge (NS 530 259; 55.5047, -4.3301), old bridge off A76 (NS 516 253; 55.4989, -4.3519),

Stair Bridge (NS 438 235; 55.4803, -4.4744), Annbank Bridge (NS 413 227; 55.4723, -4.5136), Tarholm Bridge (NS 393 221; 55.4663, -4.5449), Auchincruive Bridge (NS 388 231; 55.4751, -4.5534).

Campsites & accommodation

Coylton, on the River Coyle, and Crofthead, near Ayr, and Cumnock. Ayr is very much an old mining county, especially inland from the sea. A stay might be more pleasant in one of the seaside campsites south of Ayr in the Culzean area.

Description

Km

0   Sorn village. The river higher up has waterfalls in a forest area. Park opposite side of old stone bridge from the main road, on the verge downstream. Immediately, the river bends sharply right, then left. Weir of 2m drop just around corner, inspect from left, gentle slide.

2.5   Portage. Dangerous grade 4/5 section in flood, consisting of a sloping weir, two sheer drop weirs, and a broken weir. The portage down the left side of the river is now very difficult due to recent high fencing. Re-entry to the river is possible below the third weir, after walking inside the fence, but it might be better to start at Catrine Bridge.

3.5   Catrine village, road bridge. Access/egress at bridge is quite difficult, as it is in the middle of the village. 200m downstream, access is much easier on right side at recreation park, parking over grass on the road. Steep wooded valley, in the next 4km there are three road bridges and a railway bridge.

8   Junction with Lugar Water from left. The weir below shown on OS map has been washed away. Road bridge, Mauchline 2km on right.

9   Barskimming bridge – easier access and egress. **Warning:** Although not difficult the next 9.5km is a grade 2/3 stretch through an attractive but difficult to access/egress wooded gorge. Possible escape at Failford halfway down, on right bank. In high water, the weir just above Stair has a large wave on it.

18.5 Stair village. Access/egress at road bridge (B730).

21.5 Road bridge. Annbank village to right. Old railway bridge just before it.

25   Water of Coyle joins on left.

25.5 Road bridge. Tarholm to right.

32.5 Road bridge. Auchincruive Agricultural College to right. Rapid/broken weir at bridge could be grade 3.

121 Loch Doon

Length   Round trip of up to 16km
OS   77

Introduction

Loch Doon is hidden away high up in the trees of the Carrick Forest, but near the main A713 road, from Galloway to Ayr. It is reached by a minor road which leaves the A713 2km south of Dalmellington, and joins the loch at the north end where the River Doon exits.

Access

At north end (NS 476 014; 55.2831, -4.4022), off the road which follows the west bank, or at the southern end at Craigmalloch (NX 483 949; 55.2249, -4.3877). After this point, the road becomes a forest drive (toll road) heading west through the Carrick Forest.

Campsites & accommodation

No formal sites, wild camping in the forest.

Description

The loch is surrounded by conifers, almost Canadian in nature. It is only about 0.5km wide, and could provide entertainment for half a day.

122 River Doon

Length   7km and 10km
OS   70
Grade   1/2

Introduction

Two separate lengths of river, missing out a 10km stretch of white water in the middle, offering a useful trip if in the area.

Water Level

Easily surmised at the various bridges by looking at the small rapids.

Access

B741 bridge, near Dalmellington (NS 462 060; 55.3239, -4.4268), down to Patna bridge (NS 417 106; 55.3638, -4.5003).

The second stretch is from Dalrymple bridge (NS 359 144; 55.3960, -4.5941) to the Doonfoot bridge at Alloway (NS 326 190; 55.4362, -4.6490), with access/egress also available at Auchendrane bridge (NS 335 155; 55.4051, -4.6327).

Campsites & accommodation

Around Ayr.

Description

Upper section (7km) – The river is grade 1 or 2 for most of its length. Access near Dalmellington, as the river leaves Bogton Loch gives 7km down to Patna (egress at road bridge over river). This part of the river winds through first some boggy ground, and then grassy banks. The scenery is quite industrial, as the largest opencast coalmine in Scotland is nearby on the right bank.

Shuttle or white-water paddle – (There then follows a more difficult part of 10km to Dalrymple, grade 2/3, but grade 3+ in high water. See Scottish White Water)

Lower Section (10km) – From the put-in at Dalrymple bridge 6km of flatter water follow to Auchendrane on the A77 (limited parking),

then the final section to Doonfoot near Ayr is 4km of grade 2, with small weirs, fishing platforms, and anglers. The river is wooded and pretty for much of the way.

123 Water of Girvan

Length	21km
OS	77/76
Grade	1–2

Introduction

This is a small river, flowing from near Straiton in a long loop north, then west and south west to the sea at Girvan. From Aitkenhead down to Girven there is 21km of Grade 1–2 river, with some weirs.

Water levels

The river requires quite a good height to be paddleable (0.4m on the SEPA gauge).

Description

Km

0   Aitkenhead.

4   Crosshill.

7   B 741 road bridge.

12.5 Dailly village. There are 2 weirs on the following stretch, one 1.5km downstream of Dailly, the other just before Girvan.

21 A77 at Girvan. The paddler can either end up in the harbour at Girvan, or egress just before it to a golf course on the right bank.

Other important points

Upriver of the described section, the first 7km from Straiton is grade 3, and the river is very narrow.

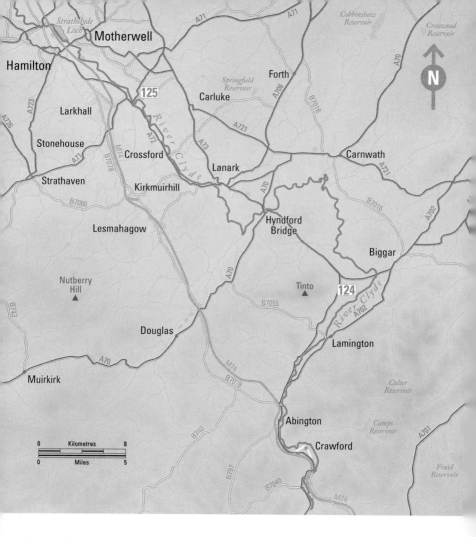

The Clyde Valley

Quothquan Law, Upper River Clyde 　　　　　　　　　　　　🔾 *Janet Moxley*

The Clyde Valley

The River Clyde has two parts of interest: a long and shallow river in its upper valley which follows the M74 for much of the way, and then below the Falls of Clyde a pleasant, slower stretch that flows nearly into Glasgow.

around New Lanark, with its Heritage Village, is well worth visiting (a World Heritage Site). The valley is also a beautiful Scottish Wildlife Trust Reserve, with badgers and peregrine falcon.

Water Level
The whole river is flat and shallow, so assessing depth of water over any bridge, especially in the higher reaches, is easy.

124 Upper River Clyde

Elvanfoot, S. Lanarkshire to Hynford Bridge, Near Lanark

Length	49km
OS	78/72
Grade	1/2 (2/3)

Introduction

The Clyde can be a good bet when water is high, but is almost impossible in low water. There are few obstructions, only some rocky rapids. It appears to be rarely paddled. The landscape is open, and often rather bare, grassy countryside, with wide open stretches that attract high winds at times. The part of the river that attracts white water paddlers, the gorge

Access

Elvanfoot Bridge (A702, NS 957 183; 55.4474, -3.6508),

Crawford Bridge (NS 952 212; 55.4734, -3.6598),

Abington Bridge (NS 934 234; 55.4927, -3.6892),

Burnfoot Bridge (NS 971 303; 55.5555, -3.6332),

Wolfclyde Bridge (near Biggar, NT 019 362; 55.6095, -3.5592),

Thankerton Bridge (NS 978 383; 55.6275, -3.6250),

Carstairs Junction Bridge (NS 956 445; 55.6827, -3.6623),

egress at Hynford Bridge (NS 914 414; 55.6540, -3.7279).

If you wish to avoid both the (permanently) closed Carstairs Junction road bridge, and the Sills of Clyde rapid at the end before Hyndford bridge, you could perhaps finish the trip at Boat road bridge (NS 978 383; 55.6275, -3.6250) near Biggar. This would cut off the last 16km of river paddling.

Note: The Sills of Clyde rapid is graded 2 or 3 depending on conditions. It is a very difficult (not recommended) portage so if you are going to do this section you have to be confident that you have the skills to run it.

Campsites & accommodation
Moffat, Crawford and Lanark.

Description
Km

0   Elvanfoot, just downstream from the joining of various burns and the Daer reservoir, which supplies most of the water. Access at the old road bridge near (east of) the motorway M74. The Navvies Graveyard on the left bank is where labourers who worked on the railway and died of typhoid in the 1800s, are buried. (There is an alternative 1km upstream, where a small track leaves the A 702 opposite the B-road to Leadhills. The track goes under the railway, and ends by a few cottages where there is parking space, and easy access on to the river).

4.5   Road bridge, and Crawford village to left. Ruined castle on right.

9   Road bridge. Abington village to left. The river now turns north-east and flows down near Biggar, one of the few towns on the whole route.

12   Duneaton Water joins left.

13   A702 road bridge at Wandel., with a grade 2 rapid just before it. Open canoes can get stuck here on rocks in low water. The scenery is now dominated by Tinto Hill (702m) to the north. About 500m downstream there is an island which is a good camping spot.

18.5   Road bridge. Lamington village to right.

26.5   A72 Wolfclyde road bridge. Biggar town 2km to right. River now widens and slows down. The next 5km is the most popular stretch for local paddling. Good views of both Tinto Hill and Quothquan Law.

31.5   Boat road bridge. Thankerton village to left, and an airstrip. The river now meanders over a very flat plain, and can be adversely affected by high winds.

40   Main railway line bridge, followed by Carstairs Junction road bridge, permanently closed to traffic as the concrete structure is dangerous, with barriers to traffic a long distance back from the river. If wishing to egress, best to leave river at the railway bridge, on river left, and it is 400m up a track to the road. Carstairs Junction (a central rail junction for Scotland) to the right.

46.5   Sills of Clyde rapid (grade 2/3). A SEPA gauging station on river right signals the start, and a wire crosses the river. 700m of bouncy water over small rock steps in high water, and a scape over ledges at low water. Carmichael Mill on river left at the end, and is the last working water mill in the area.

48.5   Hynford Bridge. Egress advised here, as Bonnington Linn (a major waterfall) is next feature, some 4km downstream. The river now changes character dramatically, to a steep-sided wooded valley.

125 Lower River Clyde
Crossford to Strathclyde Country Park

Length	18km
OS	72/64
Grade	1(2)

Crossford Bridge, Lower River Clyde   📷 *Janet Moxley*

Grade
Grade 1; Garrion Weir at NS 794 509; 55.7364, -3.9229 (which is harder in high water), grade 2 at Crossford.

Portages
Garrion Weir can be portaged on both banks.

Introduction
A useful paddle near Glasgow but in the countryside.

Water Level
Most of the river is slow and deep, and the Clyde here keeps its level for a long time after rain. A look at Crossford will tell the paddler the level.

Access
Crossford village, left bank downstream of bridge (NS 827 465; 55.6977, -3.8684).
Garrion Weir Bridge, downstream of bridge, reached by taking a dead-end down to a nursery/garden centre and parking in cul-de-sac next to roundabout up on main road (NS 793 511; 55.7382, -3.9245).
Strathclyde Park Watersports Centre (NS 730 565; 55.7851, -4.0274).
Egress at Strathclyde Park Visitor Centre (NS 719 579; 55.7974, -4.0456).

Campsites & accommodation
Lanark and Strathclyde Park.

Description
Km

0   Crossford village is some 6km downstream from Lanark. Good access on left. below bridge, which has a rock shelf under it. The countryside is pretty, with much of the Clyde Valley's soft-fruit industry here, in many glasshouses.

3   Main road, A72 on left bank.

6.5   Garrion Weir – usually the lip is blocked by trees and rubbish. Ramp on extreme right, easy shoot in moderate water. Road bridge.

15.5 River Avon joins left, followed by road bridge (A723). Entrance to Strathclyde Park (loch just over bank on right side). Water Centre on right bank. Egress either here, or...

18   Egress near Visitor Centre, onto path on right bank.

From here on, the river becomes more industrial, and egress is often difficult. There are also some large weirs.

Other important points
The water just upstream of the section described is nice, grade 2, but access is difficult.

Dumfries and Galloway

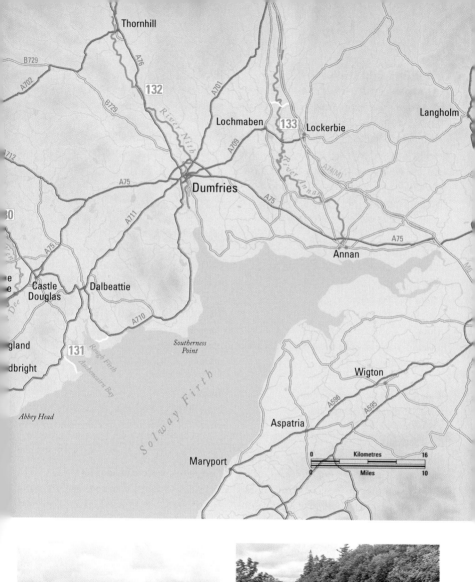

Brighouse Bay   📷 Mike Hayward

River Annan at Millhouse Bridge   📷 Jonathan Riddell

Dumfries and Galloway

This whole coast is known for fast tides, sandbanks, and exposed headlands. Short trips are possible in many of the sheltered bays. The main rivers offering any distance for paddling are the Ken/Dee, Nith and Annan. Other rivers are mainly very shallow unless in high flood. The whole area however is a delight for tourists, with an attractive coast, small villages and great stretches of forest with many walks.

126 Luce Bay

Length	21km
OS	82
Tides	See below

Tides

This trip is only possible on an ebb tide, leaving at high water.

Campsites & accommodation

Glenluce and Auchenmalg Bay.

Description

There are not many possibilities in this bay, most of it being an RAF bombing range. A coastal trip from Glenluce down to Port William is a possible safe trip in good weather (21km), but further down nearer to Burrow Head is exposed.

127 Isle of Whithorn and Garlieston

Length	12km
OS	83
Tides	See below

Tides

This trip is best done on a flood tide, leaving maybe two hours before high water.

Campsites & accommodation

Wigtown.

Description

Wigton Bay has 12km of coastline, between Isle of Whithorn and Garlieston. Both villages have safe harbours and Isle of Whithorn is a picturesque sailing centre. Further in Wigtown Bay exposes very large areas of sand and mud at low tide.

128 Gatehouse of Fleet

Length	12km
OS	83
Tides	Area dries at low water

Tides

Most of the area dries out at low water so only possible a couple of hours either side of high water.

Campsites & accommodation

Gatehouse of Fleet, Brighouse Bay, and various small caravan sites and informal/seasonal sites.

Description

A scenic bay of some 12km coastline in all, out to the Islands of Fleet to the south. Well worthwhile exploring, with the right tide and landing at one of the bays south of the southernmost island, Barlocco Isle. Airds Bay, on the south side of Fleet Bay, has landing places, a road, and a caravan site.

129 Brighouse Bay, Little Ross and Kirkcudbright Bay

Length	Round trips of 8km and 18km
OS	83
Tides	Area dries at low water

Tides

These bays dry out at low tide, and so passages should be planned to arrive on flood tides. This suggests that these trips are a maximum of 6 hours. Brighouse Bay out to Little Ross Island (a very popular trip – 8km return) is best planned by leaving on the last of the ebb, say 2 hours before low tide, with a return on the flood tide. Paddling up into Kirkcudbright Bay needs to be planned to arrive at high tide – Gulf Craig, on the west side, up to Tongland Bridge, is 5km, (10km return) so a return trip could take place between half tides both up and down. Otherwise, the paddler could be caught out on both mud and sand banks.

Introduction

This area is well known to paddlers, offering interesting possibilities for trips, especially sheltered waters for beginners, and some more challenging voyages if wished. Brighouse Bay is a long-established camp and caravan site, with a beach fronting it, ideal for learning surfing.

Access

From Brighouse Bay beach (NX 636 458; 54.7885, -4.1236).

Campsites & accommodation

Brighouse Bay, and Kirkcudbright.

Recommended short easy trip

Brighouse Bay – 2km within the bay.

Description

A trip round to Little Ross, at the mouth of Kirkcudbright Bay, can be either very straight-forward, or a problem if wind gets up. The 5km paddle in to Gull Craig is a common trip, further in to the bay being awkward with the large expanse of tidal mud.

130 Rivers Ken and Dee, and Loch Ken

Length	48km
OS	77/83
Grade	1/2(2/3)

Grade

Grade 1 and 2, but Water of Deugh grade 2/3, and Earlstoun Linn 2/3.

Portages

Several portages at dams, and sometimes over dry sections of river, see text.

Introduction

This is still a relatively little-visited area of Scotland, and offers peace and quiet and plenty of wildlife. The river and loch system offers many different types of paddling, with some awkward portages, due to the connected and complicated hydro-electric system. Turbines running usually mean water below the dams, and often in the middle of the day (apparently!). A trip could be started, if there is water, as high up as Carsphairn, but often paddling has to commence at Carsfad Loch. There are some rocky rapids below dams, and a grade 2/3 fall at Earlstoun Linn, above

Threave Castle, River Dee 📷 *Mike Hayward*

Earlstoun Loch. The river sections are generally grade 2. More suitable for an open canoe trip below Allangibbon Bridge, near St John's Town of Dalry.

It is suggested that, if camping, you stay on Loch Ken and do the river in two days.

Water Level

Paddlers have to go and look! Loch Ken and River Dee will always have enough water.

Access

Carsphairn Bridge (NX 568 930; 55.2104, -4.2530),
Kendoon (NX 601 878; 55.1647, -4.1985),
below Carsfad Loch dam (NX 604 854; 55.1432, -4.1926),
Allangibbon Bridge (NX 615 820; 55.1130, -4.1737),
Ken Bridge (New Galloway, NX 640 784; 55.0814, -4.1328),
Loch Ken viaduct (NX 684 703; 55.0098, -4.0601),

Crossmichael (NX 72 67; 54.9811, -4.0023),
Glenlochar dam (NX 732 644; 54.9581, -3.9824),
Bridge of Dee (NX 734 600; 54.9186, -3.9773).
Egress before Tongland dam (NX 703 550; 54.8729, -4.0235).

Campsites & accommodation

Loch Ken, east side, just south of Loch Ken Viaduct, and Kirkcudbright.

Recommended short easy trip

Loch Ken, from the sailing centre, up to 15km of loch.

Description

Km

0   Carsphairn. Bridge over Water of Deugh (A713). This first stretch is a rocky grade 2/3, not easy at all for open canoes.

3   Kendoon Loch.

5   Bridge over loch, halfway down. Fish farm below bridge. Dam and outflow below to right, portage to river, which may be dry. Carrying on leads to another dam in 1.5km and Gleghoul Glen, which might well also be dry! Inspect all sections below dams in advance.

7.5 Kendoon Power Station, where the two rivers join. You are now properly on the Water of Ken. Car parking probably best at Polmeddie FC car park west of road.

8.5 Carsfad Loch.

10 End of loch, dam, portage right. Water of Ken River, and rapids. Lay-by on main road below dam, very convenient for rapids.

11 Just after the Polharrow Burn joins from right, river bends left, then right, Earlstoun Linn, a two-step fall, possible with care for open canoes. Take care be-

low, as fast water follows, and there is a possible 3m fall if loch below is dry.

11.5 Earlstoun Loch.

13 End of loch, dam, long portage right.

14 Allangibbon Bridge. St John's Town of Dalry to left. Small market town. Water of Ken is now a broad river with good water. Anglers often found on this stretch. River is always paddleable below here.

20 Bridge of Ken. New Galloway 1km to right. The A713 is now on right bank all the way down Loch Ken. Scenery changes from upland wooded hills to more open agricultural land.

22 River becomes Loch Ken, almost imperceptibly. Kenmure Castle on right bank.

25.5 Loch Ken Sailing Centre on left bank. Canoes and dinghies for hire, instruction, café. This upper part of the loch is ideal for canoe sailing. Islands follow.

29.5 Ken Viaduct (disused railway line, now footpath). Power boats on this stretch, with waterskiing.

30 Campsite on left bank. Black Water of Dee joins right. Loch is now interesting, with islands, shallows and narrows. Flatter, more open scenery.

33.5 Narrows. Islands with many wading birds.

35 Crossmichael village on left bank.

37.5 Glenlochar Dam. Lift over into River Dee. Wide, deep river. No rapids.

40 Threave Island. Right channel is smaller, but passes Threave Castle. Rapid where two channels rejoin.

41 Lodge Island.

41.5 Old railway bridge, followed by main road. Threave Bridge A75, town of Castle Douglas 4km left. Rapid starts under bridge for 100m.

42 Bridge of Dee. River quietens down, is-

lands, river becomes Tongland Loch.

48 Land on right side of loch at lay-by on road, before Tongland Dam, where egress is awkward.

131 Auchencairn Bay, Orchardton Bay and Rough Firth

Length	14km
OS	84
Tides	Area dries at low water

Distances
Round trip of 14km from Rockcliffe to Auchencairn via Hestan Island.

Tides
Only possible a couple of hours either side of high water as the whole area dries out at low water.

Campsites & accommodation
Rockcliffe, Kirkcudbright, and Southerness.

Description
Possibilities for the paddler, but only near high tide. Kippford in Roughfirth is a major sailing centre, and is very sheltered.

132 Lower Nith and Estuary

Length	27 or 34.5km
OS	78/84
Grade	1–2
Tide	Estuary dries at low water

Tides
The estuary below Dumfries dries considerably at low tide. It is best to do trip down to

Glencaple on the first of an ebb tide, leaving Dumfries at high water.

Introduction

The lower, pleasant agricultural section of the Nith is usually paddled from Thornhill, giving 27km, a long day trip down to Dumfries, with the possibility of extending the trip further down the estuary.

Water Level

Fairly obvious from bridges, especially from new Dumfries by-pass bridges.

Access

Thornhill Bridge (NX 871 955; 55.2407, -3.7776),

Auldgirth Old Bridge (NX 912 864; 55.1599, -3.7096),

Dumfries Bridge above weir (NX 967 761; 55.0686, -3.6195),

Kingholm Quay (NX 975 736; 55.0463, -3.6061)

Glencaple (NX 994 685; 55.0009, -3.5746).

Campsites & accommodation

Penpont, near Thornhill, east of Dumfries on A75.

Description

Km

0 Thornhill bridge. Town to left.

4.5 Scar Water joins left. Rapids.

10.5 Barburgh Mill and main road (A76) to left.

12.5 Auldgirth Bridge.

17 Old railway bridge, weir under, probably portage left.

24 First of new by-pass bridges.

24.5 Old railway bridge, said to have metal spikes on it. Outskirts of Dumfries.

Second new by-pass bridge.

25 Third new bridge, followed by old railway bridge.

27 Dumfries town bridge, followed by a two-step weir with fish-run down left bank. Big in flood. Portage on left bank, land under bridge to inspect route.
River becomes tidal.

29.5 Kingholm Quay left. Old port for Dumfries, with warehouses.

34.5 Glencaple village left. Useful egress point. The river then widens out considerably into the Solway Firth. The Caerlaverock Nature Reserve on the left side (east) is well worth a visit.

Other important points

Upstream of the described section, the Nith is rather a strange river. It rises in Ayrshire, between Dalmellington and New Cumnock, where several burns leave a flat, wooded area that has been an opencast coal mine, then flows eastwards through flat, bleak and rather featureless countryside. It could be paddled from New Cumnock; to Kirkconnel is 15km, and a further 6.5km to Sanquhar (a former fireworks manufacturing town), where the Nith turns southwards. It is flat and winding. Then at Mennock, 4km downstream, the river changes in character and becomes white water for 11km. (See *Scottish White Water*).

133 River Annan

Length	30km
OS	78/85
Grade	1/2 and 4 weirs

Introduction

The Annan is a long, pastoral river of some 30km, flowing through the eastern part of

Dumfries-shire, now known better to travellers to Scotland as the M74 corridor. The countryside is quiet rather than especially beautiful, but with water in it the Annan would provide a day's easy paddling as an alternative to the English Lakes or the Solway coast.

It rises in the hills above Moffat, in the spectacular box canyon known as the Devil's Beeftub, is tiny through the town of Moffat, and is usually seen first by travellers at the Johnstonebridge Services on the M74, where it curls around the artificial ponds. The river can be paddled in high enough water from just below the service station, a kilometre or so down the lane on the west side of the river. Our description starts, however, from the next road bridge some 8km down, as the Annan is joined soon after by Water of Ae which nearly doubles its size. Many of the bridges have little parking, so vehicles should be left with care. The weirs can be shot with little problem in low to medium water

Water Level

A look over bridges will soon tell you if the river has water.

Access

Millhousebridge (NY 103 855; 55.1557, -3.4095),
A709 bridge (NY 106 807; 55.1126, -3.4033),
minor road bridge (NY 118 761; 55.0715, -3.3830),
Hoddom Bridge (NY 163 728; 55.0426, -3.3116),
Brydekirk Bridge (NY 187 705; 55.0224, -3.2733),
Annan Bridge (NY 191 665; 54.9865, -3.2660).

Campsites & accommodation

Lochmaben, Hoddom Castle and Annan (near the finish).

Description

Km

0   Millhousebridge, 1km west of the M74.

1.5 Applegarthtown village left bank. Ancient motte.

2   Water of Ae joins right.

4.5 The river has many bends, and a lagoon to right that is fast becoming an oxbow lake. Dryfe Water joins left.

6.5 Creamery on left bank. Road bridge (A709). Lochmaben 2km right, Lockerbie 3km left. After the bridge, the river winds, and has marshy banks for next 7km. Hightae, then Smallholm hamlets on right bank. Scenery changes to wooded.

15.5 Island, and Linn Mill left. Remains of old broken weir in low water.

16 Road bridge.

17 St Mungo's Church (historic) on left bank.

18 Mills on both banks.

19 Weir.

20.5 Water of Milk joins on left.

22.5 Hoddom Bridge. Local paddlers tend to paddle from here to Annan.

24.5 Mein Water joins left.

26 Brydekirk Bridge, village right. Weir just below bridge.

27 Large island.

28 Weir.

28.5 Annan by-pass Bridge (A75).

29.5 Road bridge, on west side of the town of Annan. Egress. River becomes tidal here.

Borders

River Teviot, the less urban bit above Hawick   📷 *Janet Moxley*

Borders

The Borders have a quite different feel to the rest of Scotland, and are often ignored by tourists rushing through to go further north. It is very agricultural, and dominated by one great river, the Tweed, which flows east from its source and watershed on the boundary between Dumfries and Galloway and Scottish Borders, near Moffat. A Tweed trip is a great journey, flowing through or near most of the. main towns, and near its end being the border of Scotland and England.

134 River Tweed

Length 110km
OS 72/75
Grade 1/2(3-)

Grades
Grade 1 and 2. Makerstoun lower rapid (-3).

Portages
Some weirs might be portaged. They are mentioned in the text.

Introduction

The Tweed is the third of the original great Scottish rivers that were seen years ago as 'the Scottish trip', or the fourth if the Dee is counted as well. There has been a feeling over the last couple of decades that the Tweed carries nothing like the water it once did, and due to the nature of the Borders, this could well be due to greater agricultural abstraction. In low water, the river is a scrape down as far as Coldstream.

The Tweed valley has many historic associations, with castles and great houses. The upper valley is beautiful and wooded, the lower after Kelso more flat and agricultural.

The river is 110km from Peebles to Berwick, offering a trip of three or four days.

Note: The 'caulds' are gently-sloping weirs, many now broken down somewhat.

Itineraries

A trip could be split thus:
Peebles to Galashiels 32km
Galashiels to Kelso 30km
Kelso to Berwick 40km
Or:

From above Peebles to Innerleithen (riverside campsite) 16km

Innerleithen to Melrose 28km

Melrose to Kelso 27km

Kelso to Berwick 40km

Recommended short easy trips

Full day trips as described above, plus Coldstream to Union Road Bridge, above Berwick – 18km.

Water Level

Look over bridges. Driving up the valley will soon tell paddlers if the river is possible without a scrape.

The tributaries of the Tweed also suffer from a lack of water for most parts of the year, and are therefore mentioned in passing. They tend to be flat and stony, and 'flashy' in nature, coming up and going down very fast. None provide any great paddling distance. The Teviot has its own entry because it does offer a couple of days' paddling.

Access

Bridge over Manor Water (NT 231 393; 55.6411, -3.2234),

Peebles bridge (NT 250 403; 55.6504, -3.1935), Innerleithen campsite (NT 340 366; 55.6185, -3.0496),

Walkerburn Bridge (NT 361 369; 55.6215, -3.0163),

Ashiesteel Bridge (NT 438 351; 55.6062, -2.8937), F

airnilee Bridge (NT 459 325; 55.5831, -2.8598), old bridge off A7 (with steps down, NT 488 323; 55.5816, -2.8138),

Melrose ford (NT 544 345; 55.6020, -2.7253),

Leaderfoot (NT 575 346; 55.6031, -2.6761),

Mertoun Bridge (NT 610 320; 55.5801, -2.6202),

Kelso riverside (above weir, NT 723 343; 55.6015, -2.4412),

A698 alongside river (NT 80 39; 55.6441, -2.3193),

Coldstream caravan site (NT 845 396; 55.6497, -2.2479),

Norham Bridge (NT 891 473; 55.7190, -2.1751),

Berwick riverside (below old bridge, NT 997 527; 55.7676, -2.0063).

Campsites & accommodation

Peebles (not on the river), Innerleithen, Galashiels (4km away, up the Gala Water, a good centre for touring the Borders), Melrose (off river), and Coldstream. Wild camping can be difficult down much of the valley. Avoid agricultural land, and look for riverside woodland or islands.

Description

The Tweed rises in the extreme south-west corner of the Borders, just over the hill from Moffat, at Tweed's Well, a very obvious spring near the A701, Moffat to Edinburgh road. It can be canoed or kayaked in high water from only a few kilometres down the road, as the valley bottom is quite flat. At Tweedsmuir road bridge is a considerable fall. A traditional place for starting trips was Stobo, about 25km downstream. However, in most summers there is not enough water from here, so distances are given from Peebles, where the river has been joined by three small tributaries.

Km

0   Peebles Bridge. Access downstream of bridge on south bank. Parking. The A72 road follows the river down the valley.

6   Cardrona, the 'new village'. New road bridge.

12 Innerleithen Bridge. Rapid. Traquair House to right. Village left.

13 Old railway bridge, and campsite left.

14 Walkerburn Cauld – can be lined down or portaged left.

15 Walkerburn Bridge. Old woollen mill, village left. Landing right below bridge.

23.5 Ashiesteel rapid, take right. Footbridge.

27 Yair Cauld, usually shootable. Inspect next kilometre, as Fairnilee rapid comes after road bridge.

27.5 Fairnilee. Well-known slalom course. A nice grade 2 rapid starting with a drop, main stream down left side. Some 200m of fast water. Lane and some parking,on left bank. Portage on left bank if desired.

30.5 Ettrick Water joins on right. River increases in size, two bridges, then faster water, with old concrete blocks in river.

(The Ettrick is a grade 2 paddle for 10km from the bridge below Ettrickbridge, Colin's bridge, 5km above Selkirk, down through Selkirk to join the Tweed. It is a grade 3 above this. There are some rocky rapids, a cauld at the junction of the Yarrow and a broken weir below Selkirk Bridge. The Yarrow has a grade 3 gorge not far up from the confluence.)

33 Abbotsford House (Sir Walter Scott's) to right. Landing and picnic place on left. Abbotsford bridge (main A6091 road). Borders General Hospital 3km right. Gala Water joins left. Galashiels Town 2km left.

35.5 Road bridge.

37 Melrose Cauld. Steep and rocky, can be shot left when enough water. Portage left. Footbridge below, access/egress to Melrose right, Gattonside to left.

40.5 A68 road bridge. Old railway viaduct just before. Egress on right just above bridge, on to minor road. River Leader joins left. (The Leader gives a fast 9km run from the A68 bridge between Lauder and Earlston down a pleasant valley, near the main road all the way). Rapid just below confluence. Scott's View, and Monument, very visible on hill on left bank for some distance.

45.5 Dryburgh footbridge. Dryburgh Abbey left.

46 Island, rock ledges and shallows below. Old campsite to left.

49 Merton Cauld. Shoot centre, or portage right. Bridge, B6404. Parking east side. River broadens out, islands.

55.5 Rutherford Cauld. Left side to shoot, considerable waves, right at island below.

58 Makerstoun House on left bank signals approach to Makerstoun rapids, most difficult on Tweed. If water is low, this stretch will take some time. Upper and Middle Makerstoun rapids have a route through on the right sides, quite difficult to see at times, easier in high water. Lower Makerstoun rapid is appearing when the drop appears ahead.

60 Lower Makerstoun rapid presents little problem for kayaks, but is tricky for open canoes… inspect. The usual route in medium water is down the extreme right side, down 4 drops, with the last very narrow, requiring some skill. In high to very high water, there is a route down the left side of the river. River now quietens down considerably.

63 Floors Castle to left.

64 Kelso Cauld can be difficult, shoot on right in high water. Inspect.
River Teviot joins right (See Route 135).

65 Road bridge. Most of town to left. Usual services. Cauld just after.

70.5 Banff Mill weirs. Two main drops, three channels. Best route is left side of river for first drop, and a tight turn to right, and down centre channel. Keeping to the left channel would entail two rocky drops. Inspect from left bank if not sure. Water heavy if river is high.

75.5 Carham Cauld, there is usually a route to shoot, seen easily from the water

77 Island, take right channel.

79.5 Cauld – shoot centre.

82 Approaching Coldstream. Caravan site left.

82.5 Coldstream bridge. Town to the left.

83.5 Cauld, route on right. River is now slow and deep, islands.

93 Road bridge, B6470, Norham village right.

100.5 Union road bridge. River becomes tidal.

106.5 Berwick, road and rail bridges, town to the left.

135 River Teviot

Length	50km
OS	74/79/80
Grade	1/2(3)

Introduction

The Teviot is included as it offers a fair distance of good paddling (2 days), and is the largest of the Tweed tributaries. A trip down Teviot and Tweed would give 4 days of paddling, a lovely trip. It is also close to main roads for much of the way.

The river rises in forest to the south-west of Hawick, and can be paddled from the aptly-named village of Teviothead, in high water. The river here is small, with overhanging trees, but possible in an open canoe with care. The stretch of 4–5km through Hawick itself is the most tricky (with a continuous section of grade 2 white water, with three sections that

Lunch stop, River Tweed 　　📷 *Mary Connacher*

can reach grade 3) but the rest is a grade 1/2, with pleasant and frequent rapids. The Hawick section can be tricky in flood, as the river runs very fast. The countryside is pretty all the way. **Note:** The 'caulds' are gently-sloping weirs, many now broken down somewhat.

Water Level

Judge from the level through Hawick. If there is enough water here, the rest of river will be fine, but the higher reaches could still be shallow. They will need inspection.

Access

Teviothead (NT 408 058; 55.3427, -2.9350),
Martinshouse Bridge, above Hawick (NT 482 134; 55.4118, -2.8198),
campsite off A698 (NT 534 169; 55.4437, -2.7382),
Ancrum bridge (NT 639 237; 55.5057, -2.5731),
Kalemouth Bridge (NT 708 274; 55.5394, -2.4643),
Kelso Bridge (NT 727 336; 55.5953, -2.4348).

Campsites & accommodation

Camping can be had just below Hawick, near Jedburgh on the River Jed, or as for River Tweed.

Description

Km

0   Teviothead. Small car park about 1km downstream of village, on left side alongside river. The A7 is a very busy road, take care. Overhanging trees down to Hawick.

4   River passes under the A7 to the south side.

7.5 Newmill. Minor road bridge. Pub and telephone to left.

11   Branxholm Bridgend - river passes under road to north side. Joined by Borthwick Water from left and the flow increases.

12   Martin's Bridge. Start of faster and shallower section.

13   Rugby pitches on left - keep right of island, many bushes and obstructions, especially supermarket trolleys. River becomes quite urban.

14   Hawick Cauld. Weir is safe to shoot, but avoid the salmon steps in the middle. Start of continuous grade 3 section. Portage on left bank.

      Note: There are high flood defence walls through Hawick and this can mean a very long swim if you come out of your boat in high water.

14.5 First road bridge.

15   Main Hawick road bridge, centre of town. River fast and straight, old woollen mills on banks.

17.5 Small weir, bend, bushes in river, (keep right), sharp bend, then 60m of rocky water with waves, small fall, stone bridge, and egress at campsite on right bank.

21   Road comes alongside river on left bank – egress, and some parking.

23   Road bridge, Denholm village on right bank.

Hawick, River Teviot   📷 *Janet Moxley*

26   Rule Water joins right. Long, slow and winding stretch now to A68 road.

31.5 Ale Water joins from the left.

32.5 A68 road bridge. Access upstream under old bridge. Jedburgh is 5km to right. Harestanes Estate both banks.

33.5 Easy sloping weir.

34.5 Footbridge, followed by broken-down cauld.

35   River Jed joins from the right. (The Jed is a kayaking river in high water, with two high weirs in Jedburgh.)

37   Nisbet road bridge, village left.

42   Kalemouth Bridge, Kale Water joins right. Bend to left, then a broken weir, followed by trees.

43   Island.

44   Weir, small drop, easy to shoot.

45   Old railway bridge, now a footpath.

45.5 Weir.

46   Weir.

48.5 Long, straight stretch, followed by broken cauld. Castle on high left bank, with River Tweed on the other side. Sharp bend to right heralds a grade 2 section, islands, rocky water, road bridge, a weir, and the last stretch down to the Tweed.

50   Junction with River Tweed.

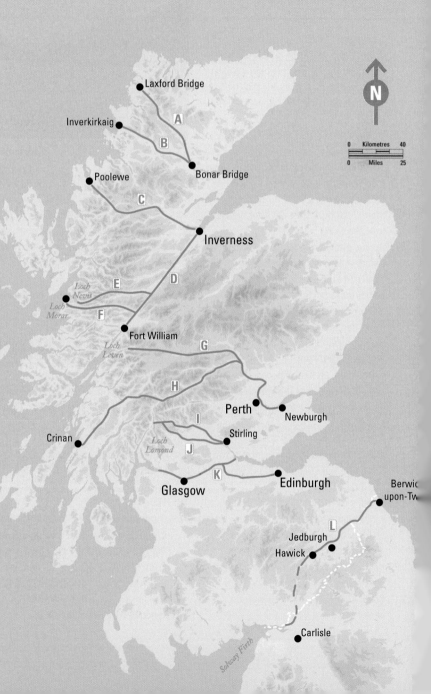

Cross Scotland Routes

Contents

Loch Stack and Arkle 📷 *Mike Forrester*

Cross Scotland Routes

All of the routes in this section are quite long and serious expeditions, although the two 'low level' routes have the advantage of being both sheltered from the worst of the weather, and being nearer to habitation and help. The canal route across the Central Belt of Scotland can also be quite urban in places, and the Great Glen passage is probably the most-paddled holiday in Scotland. Those who have achieved it will also have a quiet smile when remembering heavy weather on Loch Ness, 'shelter from bad weather' being a relative description!

Apart from those two, the other routes across Scotland can be quite a challenge, with boggy portages, heat and midges in high summer, and usually a stiff climb up from the west coast to the watershed. Some are indeed quite mad, and are not recommended for pleasure!

Paddlers are warned that, in most places, the terrain means that canoe trolleys can't be used for portaging, and that it can be treacherous underfoot. Lining up or down watercourses can also be well-nigh impossible. A best plan would be for paddlers to carry all their gear in rucksacks, and therefore be free to carry canoes or kayaks. If not, an expedition might be forced into several journeys over the most problematic stretches.

Whilst the carrying of mobile phones can be a safety measure, as can back-up crews, please remember that mobile phone masts are not erected in the mountains on the watershed, where help might be most needed. Signal strength is not assured. Finally and cheerfully, Scotland is famous for very changeable weather. This can quite well mean snow showers on midsummer day. All in all, the message is that expedition groups must be self-sufficient, carrying all necessary food, water and clothing.

The routes are described from the north of Scotland to the south, and only bare details are given. Detailed planning with maps must allow for distances, features and obstacles. Routes through peat bogs, and river features such as weirs and walkways etc. do change over time. Follow the Scottish Access Code with regard to rough camping, take only photos and leave only footprints.

A Laxford Bridge to Bonar Bridge

Length	72.5km
OS	9/15/16
Grade	2

Introduction

A route commencing in one of the most spectacular parts of the north, with views of the quartzite Arkle and Foinaven to the east, Loch Laxford is a good place to start. The height of this route is not a problem, as a main road follows it all of the way, but the long easterly drag down Loch Shin to the east is not one of Scotland's finest bits of scenery.

Description

The purist wishing to complete a coast to coast route will start at Laxford Bridge and portage their craft for 4.5km up the A838 following the course of the grade 3/4 River Laxford until they reach Lochstack Lodge: the more sane will commence their journey from Lochstack Lodge. Loch Stack is a lovely 3.5km to the end, with Ben Stack a beautiful conical mountain to the south. You then have a 1km portage up the road to Loch nan Ealachan, under a bridge to Loch More, which is 1km long.

Then another 3.5km portage up the road to Loch Merkland, (you cross the watershed at 144m). Loch Merkland is 4.5km, and now you may be able to paddle 2km downhill on the Merkland River (some rapids). Loch a' Ghriama (2.5km) follows, an offshoot of Loch Shin, then this main and very long loch of 27km. Loch Shin does feel as if it's never going to end, and it has relatively few features. Very much a fishing loch, you will meet many small boats.

Lairg is a welcome break, the only town on this route, and then a choice: a long road portage, or the River Shin. The former is 12km by road to Invershin Station, on the Kyle of Sutherland; the alternative is an attempt at parts of the river, with often no water, including the Falls of Shin. Getting in and out of the river gorge is not easy.

Then follows 5km of tidal water to Bonar Bridge.

Other important points

Total distance:	72.5km.
Time required:	Probably 4 days.

B Inverkirkaig to Bonar Bridge

Length	67.5km
OS	15/16/21
Grade	1/2/3

Introduction

This is a difficult and not recommended route. It was paddled to join up two quite reasonable canoeing areas, the Inverpolly Nature Reserve area in the west, north of Ullapool, and the River Oykel/Kyle of Sutherland route in the east.

Ascending Kinlochewe River   📷 *Jonny Hawkins*

Description

From Inverkirkaig, a few miles south of Lochinver, the route goes up the River Kirkaig (see *Scottish White Water*) valley. The valley is beautiful, but the portage is fairly tough, some 3km to the Falls, and a further 1km to the Fionn Loch, up an often wet, muddy, and stony track. Then follows a lovely 11km through Fionn Loch, the connecting short river, and Loch Veyatie to the waterfall at the top. A further 3km round to the Ledmore River, which is flat, and can usually be paddled upstream 4.5km to Loch Borralan. The idea of the route then ends up with a problem, as the burn coming down is impossible to line. It is a portage of 4.5km to the Allt Eileag (grade 3, see *Scottish White Water*) over the watershed access to the Oykel. When I did this, we had no idea of the steepness of the river and ended up in a diffi-cult and hard portage (mostly) 1.5km from the road down to the Oykel. The other alternative is a portage of 12km to Lubcroy. The river has a slow 8km down to Lubcroy; rapids from grade 1 to grade 3, fast if one has nerves in high water, otherwise some portages and wading.

Lubcroy to a point by the river alongside a Highland Council Roads depot, 2km. A portage along the road for 1km to Oykel Bridge and hotel avoids a white water stretch including the Falls of Oykel.

The paddler will be pleased to know that from here, it is all straightforward to the sea at Bonar Bridge (tidal before this point), 28km. (See Route 028).

Other important points

Total distance: 67.5km.

Time required: Probably 4 days at least.

C Loch Maree to Conon Bridge

Length	85.5km
OS	20/25/26
Grade	1–2

Outline

Loch Maree, River Bran and River Conon to Conon Bridge.

Introduction

This is a reported route, second-hand from writing on a bothy wall, with only initials, not a full name. As the start and finish have been done many times, there is no reason to suspect it.

Description

See Route 024, for Loch Maree. The loch is portaged alongside the River Ewe, up from Poolewe, for 1km, then Loch Maree is 21km long. A portage of 3km up to Kinlochewe is followed by a further portage of 8km over the watershed to Loch a' Chroisg.
See Route 031 for the rest of the route down the lochs to the River Bran and on to the River Conon.

Other important points

Total distance: 85.5km.
Time required: Probably 5 days, so as not to hurry Loch Maree, to account for the long central portage, and for the lower portages.

D Great Glen (Caledonian Canal)

Length	92km
OS	26/34/41
Grade	-

Introduction

This is deservedly a very popular route across Scotland, but it is still quite possible to paddle for three or four days and not see another canoe outside of the midsummer holiday period. It is a voyage almost at sea level, with great scenery all the way, and the safety of a canal with traffic and a main road. It is still possible, however, to find both places for stops on the way where there is peace and quiet and wild camping spots. The latter are, however, becoming less easy to find.
Scottish Canals control the canal, and the very good website has many practical details about the canal (www.scottishcanals.com).

Description

The route is 96.6km long (60 miles), of which 35.4km (22miles) is man-made. The Caledonian Canal is one of the great waterways of the world, sharing characteristics with both the Gota Canal in Sweden and the Rideau Canal in Canada, both of which it is twinned with.
Designed by Thomas Telford, the canal was built between 1803 and 1822. It has four aqueducts over burns (one being the canoeable though small Loy), 29 locks, and 10 bridges. The route passes along Loch Lochy, Loch Oich, Loch Ness, and Loch Dochfour.
A 'normal' time for a passage by canoe is three days, which can obviously be extended with sightseeing. Large boats using the locks are told it will take them a minimum of 14 hours

over two days. The locks only work during a normal working day, 8.00 until 6.00pm in summer, and are worked by Scottish Canals staff. Plan to portage around the locks, some of which are long flights, although you might just be able to attach yourself to a friendly motor cruiser.

The route is described from south to north, as this is the usual way of the prevailing wind, but it can change! The lochs can all build up large waves in high wind, so be prepared to either stop, or to paddle close to one of the banks.

There are various formal campsites along the glen, some on the water, and some places are mentioned as having rough camping possibilities.

Km

0   Fort William/Corpach. Canal, the Neptune's Staircase series of locks stretch for 2.5km.

12.5 Gairloch swing bridge. Entrance to Loch Lochy. River Lochy leaves on right after 250m, and then the River Arkaig enters on left after 3.5km. Loch Lochy is 15km long.

27.5 The loch narrows, yacht moorings on right, then on left. Canal.

28   Laggan locks. Small village and B&Bs to right.

30.5 Laggan swing bridge. Entrance to Loch Oich. Loch Oich is wooded and extremely pretty, 6km long. Great Glen Water Park on right, accommodation and camping.

34   On left side, Invergarry Castle, Glengarry Hotel, and then the mouth of River Garry. Just after this on left, possibilities for camping in marshy woodland. This loch has buoyage for larger boats as it is relatively shallow and narrow.

36.5 End of loch, Bridge of Oich, road swing-bridge. River Oich leaves left over a weir.

Keep to the canal, as the river is grade 1 and 2, and often shallow. Canal to Fort Augustus

37.5 Collochy Lock.

40.5 Kytra Lock.

44   Fort Augustus locks. Plan to have a break here, as the carry down these locks will leave you exhausted. Often a busy place, where the world stops to watch people in boats hitting each other and the lock walls. Town with shops and cafés etc. Exit to Loch Ness, a wondrous sight, as it stretches to the horizon, all 36km of it! The right bank, the quieter side of Loch Ness, has many camping possibilities, squeezed in for most of its length between the shore and a B-road. The left bank has few places.

51   Rubha Ban campsite on left bank.

52   Invermoriston to left.

60   Foyers village to right.

64   Inverfarigaig to right.

69   Urquhart Castle on left bank, followed by Urquhart Bay on left. There are camping possibilities here, and much wooded and marshy ground. On the right side of the loch there are many picnic sites.

75.5 Camp and caravan site on right bank.

78   Tore Point, loch narrows.

80.5 Lochend village on left side. Loch Ness becomes the narrower Loch Dochfour.

82.5 River Ness leaves right (grade 1/2 with weirs). The normal route stays on the canal.

83.5 Dochgarroch village left. Campsite.

89.5 Canal and river which have been running parallel part company – two campsites.

91   Muirtown Locks.

92   Canal leaves Muirtown Basin into the sea.

Approaching Fort Augustus Lochs   ⌷ *Eddie Palmer*

E Loch Nevis to Great Glen

Length	131km
OS	33/34/26
Grade	1/2

Outline
Loch Nevis, River Carnoch, Loch Quoich and River Garry to Great Glen.

Introduction
This is again a reported route, a variation of the Great Glen, using the Garry system from the west coast, but with a very tough carry over the western watershed.

Description
The route commences from the head of Loch Nevis, with a paddle in from either Mallaig, or along Loch Morar (see Routes 045 and 046). The route is from the north-east exit from the loch at Camusory, up the River Carnach. The river might be paddled or lined for a distance up, but after 2km or so the gradient steepens. It is 7km up to a small loch, the 1km Lochan nam Breac, then a final 1.5km rocky dribble to Loch Quoich, over 200m climb vertically.

The lochs of Glen Quoich and Glen Garry then follow (see Route 053) for 36km to the River Garry, to be portaged (5km) as far as Loch Oich. The Great Glen – Route D above – is then followed to Inverness (58km).

Other important points
Total distance:
129km (Loch Morar route).
131km (Loch Nevis route from Mallaig).

Loch Morar   📷 *Jonny Hawkins*

Time required: This must take at least 6 days, and could take considerably more. The terrain for the main portage is very hard, and this route is one of the longest across Scotland.

F Loch Morar to Great Glen

Length	128km
OS	33/40/41
Grade	2+(4+)

Outline
Loch Morar, Glen Pean, Loch Arkaig to Loch Lochy and Great Glen.

Introduction
This is again a variation of the route above, with the ascent made from the head of Loch Morar, instead of Loch Nevis.

Description
The approach is as Route 046, and then Glen Pean is taken almost due east from the south-east end of the loch. The unnamed glen has a 2.5km climb up to the bealach, to a height of 120m, and is noteworthy for the giant rock, 'Noah's Ark', which guards the entry to Glen Pean. The burn down here is small for 4.5km, passing through a large lochan on the way down. It is then joined by numerous tiny water courses near a bothy and a ruin, and becomes a larger river that may be paddled. It is a further 5.5km to Loch Arkaig.

Loch Arkaig (Route 055) is 19km long, and the 2km River Arkaig (one portage, grade 4+), leads down to Loch Lochy in the Great Glen. From this point to Inverness is 76km.

Other important points
Total distance:	128km.
Time required:	Probably 5–6 days.

Loch Leven from the Kinlochleven end   📷 *Tony Hammock*

G Kinlochleven to Perth

Length	128km
OS	41–43/53
Grade	2/3(4)

Outline

Kinlochleven to Perth via Blackwater Reservoir, Rannoch Moor, River Gaur, Loch Rannoch, River Tummel and River Tay.

Introduction

This is a very hard, though rewarding cross-country route, at 325m height, the highest route of this group. It also has some of the toughest portages.

Description

The trip starts at Kinlochleven at the head of Loch Leven (Route 060), off Loch Linnhe. There is immediately a horrific climb, from sea level up to the Blackwater Reservoir, the highest the expedition will go, in just 6.5km. The one saving grace of this path, starting as a forest track, is that it becomes a concrete cover over the outflow from the dam after 2.5km, and the canoe trolley will hum along over this.

(This fact was kept secret by several writers of the route in the past). This climb will take half a day, and the dam provides a greatly scenic campsite, surrounded by mountains, so using a first afternoon or evening for this part is maybe a good plan, as recovery time will be needed.

The Blackwater Reservoir is 12.5km long, and the height often means that a sail across here is quite likely in the prevailing westerlies.

The problems really start at the eastern end. It is only about 6.5km as the crow flies east, then south to Rannoch Station, but the route-finding and terrain can make grown men weep! The river is shallow, rock-strewn and winding, and so any lining-up can be forgotten. The only answer is to carry the canoe or kayak over uneven ground, trying to remember where one is going. After a time, the railway line comes invitingly near to the north, but beware – it is first of all illegal to walk on the line, and secondly, you might know the times of the passenger trains but you won't know when freight trains are coming! There are also snow tunnels here – bad to meet a train in a snow tunnel.

Once reaching Rannoch Station, you are on the way downhill, with the hotel and café beckoning.

Rannoch Moor

The next obstacle is that, after paddling on to Dubh Lochan and Loch Laidon (1km), and finding the river exit, the Garbh Ghaoir – 3km, can be a mite difficult. Immediately, two grade 2/3 rapids follow, the second under the railway bridge, and then an appreciable drop as a good grade 3 takes you 800m down to Loch Eigheach. At least you get 2km of flat paddling, then over the dam (either side) down onto the road to Loch Rannoch. The River Gaur poses a problem. It has some easy water, but one grade 4 rapid, seen after 2km down the road, and also at least two places of rocky grade 3. The only real solution is to walk – a portage of 4km to Bridge of Gaur. At this bridge, access can be had onto the end of the river just before it joins Loch Rannoch.

The rest of the route is covered in Routes 089, 090 and 098.

Other important points

The distances are:

Kinlochleven to Rannoch Station – 26km.

Rannoch Station to Pitlochry – 57.5km.

Pitlochry to Perth – 54.5km.

Total distance: 138km.

Time required: Could be completed by the very fit in 3 days (the Tay is very fast), but a more sensible target is 4–5 days.

H Crinan to Newburgh

Length	220km
OS	55, 50, 51, 52, 53
Grade	1 to 3

Outline

Crinan Canal on the west coast, via a portage to Loch Awe, and then roads to the Tay watershed, and down to the east coast via the River Dochart, Loch Tay, and River Tay.

Introduction

A new route accomplished in 2020 by Jonathan Kitching from Aboyne, Aberdeenshire, to raise funds for three charities including his local hospice. He used a bike and trailer for the three portages, which he carried in his open canoe.

Description

The paddling on this route is fairly straight-forward, being canal, loch, river, loch and river, but the portages by road are quite demanding. The road from Dalmally to Tyndrum rises by 250m, and then drops down to Crianlarich.

Distances

Crinan to Bellanoch – 4km
Bellanoch to Ford (Loch Awe) – 15km
Loch Awe – Ford to near Dalmally – 35km
Road portage. Dalmally to Crianlarich via A85 and A82 – 29km
River Dochart, Crianlarich to Killin –21km
Killin to Kenmore – (Loch Tay) – 24km
Kenmore to Caputh (River Tay) – 47km
Caputh – Newburgh (River Tay and estuary) – 45km

Other important points

Total distance: 220km
The paddler concerned took 6 days, but 5 is quite possible.
The main road portage is on very busy A roads, and is advised to be tackled in the early morning in summer.

Loch Long to Stirling

Length	63km
OS	56/57
Grade	1/2(3-)

Outline

Lochs Long, Lomond, Arklet, Katrine, Achray and Venachar to Stirling.

Introduction

This is a lovely route, and was probably first made in the 1950s. Possibly the sight of the tourist steamer on Loch Katrine proved a temptation, as before the Scottish Outdoor Access Code, the loch was illegal to paddle, being a reservoir. The middle sections of small river and loch can also be very dry. From Callander, the river route is one of the easiest in this section.

Description

Loch Long and Loch Lomond are covered in Routes 075 and 076. At Arrochar is a short portage of about 3.5km from Arrochar over the hill and main road to Tarbert, and into Loch Lomond. It is then a paddle of 5km up to Inversnaid. From here it is a portage of 2km to Loch Arklet, which is 4km long. The road over to Loch Katrine is 1.5km down to Stronachlachar pier. Loch Katrine is 9km down to its end at the road over to Loch Achray, and a portage is required of 1.5 km to bypass the dry Achray Water. The way to Loch Achray is over the main A 821 road; the loch has some lovely campsites on the wooded banks.

Loch Achray is 2km long, with the small River Black Water leading into Loch Venacher. From here the route is Route 114 down to Stirling. Once on the River Teith progress is a lot faster.

Awaiting the Falkirk Wheel, Union Canal   📷 *Sonya Anderson*

Other important points

Total distance: 63km.

Time required: 3 days minimum, probably four.

J Loch Long to River Forth and Stirling

Length	82km
OS	56/57
Grade	1

Outline

Lochs Long, Lomond, Arklet, Chon, and Ard to River Forth and Stirling.

Introduction

This is a variation of Route I above and leaves Route I after Loch Arklet, taking the B829 south towards Aberfoyle. It includes the small Lochs Arklet and Chon. From Aberfoyle, the Forth and Teith takes the paddler across Scotland.

Description

Loch Long and Loch Lomond are Routes 075 and 076. As for Route I, it is 16km to the eastern end of Loch Arklet. Then the route turns south, portage of 4km to Loch Chon, and this loch provides 3.5km of paddling through a small river to Loch Dhu. Off onto the road again for 2.5km down to Loch Ard. These two sections of road need care in the summer as they are very busy (perhaps best to do the portages in an evening). Loch Ard, however, is a delight. The River Forth commences, very shallow at first, through Milton to Aberfoyle and then the River Forth is followed, see Route 115.

Other important points

Total distance: 82km.

Time required: 3 days (more if you take your time on the Forth).

K Glasgow to Edinburgh

Length	103km
OS	64/65/66

Outline
Glasgow to Edinburgh, via the Forth and Clyde Canal, and Union Canal.

Description
These two canals are described in Routes 118 and 119. Planning would have to include an overnight stop, either as described for wild camping or by leaving the canal, or even by staying somewhere comfortable, possibly near Falkirk if going west to east.

Other important points
Total distance: 103km.
Time required: 2 days minimum.

L Solway Firth to Berwick

Length	103km
OS	85,79,80,74 and 75
Grade	1/2(3-)

Outline
Solway Firth via Teviot and Tweed to Berwick.

Introduction
This is the craziest route by far, and came out of a bet the author had years ago just after a couple of open canoe luminaries had circumnavigated Wales (work that out!).

Description
I had the idea of paddling and sailing around the south of Scotland. From Edinburgh to Glasgow was easy enough, but the border presented a new problem. So, one day I and a companion set out, luckily with a support crew. We sailed up the 24km of the Solway from Southerness, west of Dumfries on a high flood tide (this was the best bit), and managed to paddle up the Border Esk as far as Longtown (8km from the river mouth). Trying to paddle/line up/drag the canoe further up proved rather difficult, and so after another 7km we left the river below Canonbie.

We then gave in with exhaustion, and portaged the canoes (by car) the 33km up to Teviothead, but then did make the whole journey down the Teviot and Tweed.

For the Teviot and Tweed, see Routes 127 and 128.

Other important points
Total distance: 140km.
Time required: Endless, but at least 5 days.

L

M

N

O

P

Q

R

S

T

U

V

W